# MONSTERS
## AND VILLAINS

D0570241

# MONSTERS
## AND VILLAINS
### OF THE MOVIES AND LITERATURE

GERRIE McCALL

an imprint of

**SCHOLASTIC**
www.scholastic.com

Copyright © 2008 Amber Books Ltd

All rights reserved. No part of this work may be reproduced, stored
in a retrieval system, or transmitted in any form or by any means,
electronic, mechanical, photocopying, recording, or otherwise,
without the prior permission of the copyright holder.

an imprint of
■SCHOLASTIC
www.scholastic.com

Scholastic and Tangerine Press and associated logos are trademarks
of Scholastic Inc.

Published by Tangerine Press, an imprint of Scholastic Inc.;
557 Broadway, New York, NY 10012

Scholastic Canada Ltd.
Markham, Ontario

Scholastic Australia Pty. Ltd.
Gosford NSW

Scholastic New Zealand Pty. Ltd.
Greenmount, Auckland

Scholastic UK
Coventry, Warwickshire

Grolier International Inc
Makati City, Philippines

10 9 8 7 6 5 4 3 2

ISBN-10: 0-545-07938-1
ISBN-13: 978-0-545-07938-9

Editorial and design by
Amber Books Ltd
Bradley's Close
74–77 White Lion Street
London N1 9PF
United Kingdom
www.amberbooks.co.uk

Project Editor: Michael Spilling
Design: Tony Cohen
Illustrations: Myke Taylor/The Art Agency

Printed in Singapore

**Picture credits:**
All illustrations by Myke Taylor/The Art Agency © Amber Books Ltd.

# Contents

# Introduction

The earliest tribes of prehistoric humans were convinced there was something dangerous out there in the dark, and there have always been monsters and villains in every culture ever since. Humankind's natural curiosity draws us to the unknown, and so primitive Man told stories around the fire about bizarre creatures and dangerous spirits. Ancient peoples, from Greece to Norway, scared each other with sagas involving terrible monsters in epic struggles between good and evil. Heroes did battle against horrible creatures and, with the help of the gods, usually triumphed. Fear is a deep and powerful emotion. Fans of horror who seek out villains and monsters face their deepest fears, and it is true we need to understand evil in order to know how to protect ourselves against it. We also need reassurance that good will win out in the end. Villains and monsters allow ordinary people the opportunity to rise to the occasion and show the best in themselves by defeating those dark forces that threaten their lives and their values.

Vampires, ghosts, zombies, cannibals, creatures risen from the grave, wild beasts, and strange forces of nature all allow us to explore the dark side of our imaginations and confront our fear of death. Every monster's story contains a lesson in how to deal with those who try to harm us. Whether the evil is hiding in the dark ready to pounce or hunting us down, there are methods for conquering what scares us.

One of the best things about villains and monsters is that they entertain us. They provide us with the excitement of being frightened and they do things that we would never dare to do. They remind us of the difference between right and wrong. But some people worry that they might not recognize evil. This book is a guide to some of the greatest villains and monsters throughout history. Inside lurk the creatures that people fear most. The awful beast, the remorseless killer, the supernatural, and the just plain wicked are at their most enjoyable when they can safely be shut away in a book.

# Werewolf

**EARS**
The large, pointed ears hear the faintest sounds made by prey from a great distance.

**EYES**
Keen, merciless eyes can spot victims even in the shadows.

**MOUTH**
A bloodcurdling howl salutes the moon and warns that the werewolf's hunt is beginning. Its fangs subdue prey and shred meat from bones easily.

**BODY**
Built for endurance, the muscular body stalks and chases as long as the full moon is shining.

**PAWS**
Strong hands and feet grip anything in this beast's path. The claws tear away any flesh not already slashed by the fangs.

Werewolves are humans with the ability to shift their shape into wolves. During the day, they are ordinary people, but a full moon triggers a terrible transformation. The person's body sprouts hair, grows fangs, and enlarges into its werewolf form. Prowling only at night, it devours cattle, kidnaps children, attacks travelers, and destroys what it cannot eat. Once it tastes human blood, it is forever cursed. A person may not know he or she is a werewolf. The only clue may be repeated nightmares of pursuing humans through the woods at night. Immune to aging and disease, the werewolf must eat the flesh of the living for all eternity.

SIZE

▶ ANYONE CAN BECOME A WEREWOLF by rubbing his or her body with a magic potion, drinking water from the footprint of a werewolf, eating wolf's brains, sleeping under the full moon on a Friday, having two werewolf parents, or being bitten by a werewolf. Unlike the vampire, it cannot be harmed or frightened away by religious artifacts. The only way to kill a werewolf is with a silver bullet. The dead werewolf's head must be cut off and burned so that it does not return as a vampire three days later.

## Where in the world?

**Werewolves are prevalent worldwide. In any country you visit, you may encounter a werewolf in the dark.**

## Did you know?

● Some believe that children born on December 24 will become werewolves.

● A poisonous herb called *wolfsbane* can be used to ward off a werewolf.

● Injuries suffered while in wolf form will show on the skin when the werewolf returns to human form.

● The mere touch of silver to a werewolf's skin can cause burns and scarring.

● In Argentina, the belief that a seventh son would become a werewolf was so strong that many parents abandoned or killed their seventh sons. To stop this practice, a law was passed in 1920, which stated that the president of Argentina is the official godfather of every seventh son born in the country. The state awards seventh sons scholarships, and they receive gold medals at their baptisms.

# The Creature from the Black Lagoon

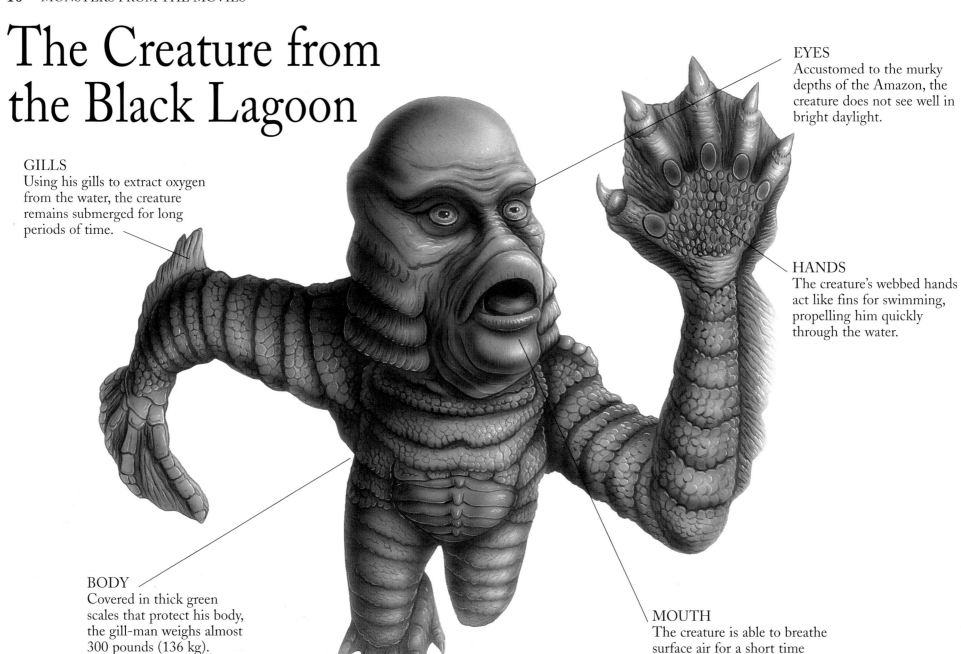

**GILLS**
Using his gills to extract oxygen from the water, the creature remains submerged for long periods of time.

**EYES**
Accustomed to the murky depths of the Amazon, the creature does not see well in bright daylight.

**HANDS**
The creature's webbed hands act like fins for swimming, propelling him quickly through the water.

**BODY**
Covered in thick green scales that protect his body, the gill-man weighs almost 300 pounds (136 kg).

**MOUTH**
The creature is able to breathe surface air for a short time before returning to the water.

Scientists visiting South America discover the skeletal hand of a half-man, half-fish creature with webbed fingers. Hoping to find the rest of the fossilized skeleton, they embark on an expedition to the Black Lagoon, a remote place from which no one has ever returned. It is home to a frightening creature more than 15 million years old: the only survivor of a species of gill-men. Though he spends most of his time underwater, he is capable of walking upright on land. His webbed hands are adapted for swimming, but they are strong enough to strangle a man.

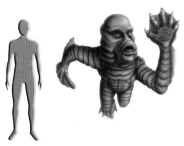

SIZE

► A BEAUTIFUL WOMAN WHO IS PART OF THE SCIENTIFIC EXPEDITION fascinates the creature. When she goes swimming in the lagoon, she is unaware that he is following her. The gill-man becomes tangled in underwater ropes attached to the boat's dragnet as the woman swims away. The single claw he leaves stuck in the net lets the scientists know just how close they came to him. The crew uses a poisoned dart to temporarily paralyze the gill-man so they can capture him.

## Where in the world?

AMAZON

**With the largest drainage basin of any river in the world, the Amazon provides countless hiding places for the prehistoric gill-man.**

## Did you know?

● In another failed attempt to capture the gill-man, a member of the crew wounds him with a spear gun. The angry creature takes revenge by killing one of the scientists. When they do manage to capture him, the gill-man escapes from the tank in which he has been placed.

● Furious about being held captive in a tank, the gill-man attacks his guard and would kill him if not for the woman onboard. She strikes the creature with a lantern, driving him away.

● The creature kidnaps the woman, taking her to his hidden cavern. The crew rescues her by firing bullets into the creature and stabbing him with a knife.

● The gill-man's normal diet is fish. He does not eat humans, but will kill them when provoked. He attacks when prying scientists disturb his habitat.

# Imhotep

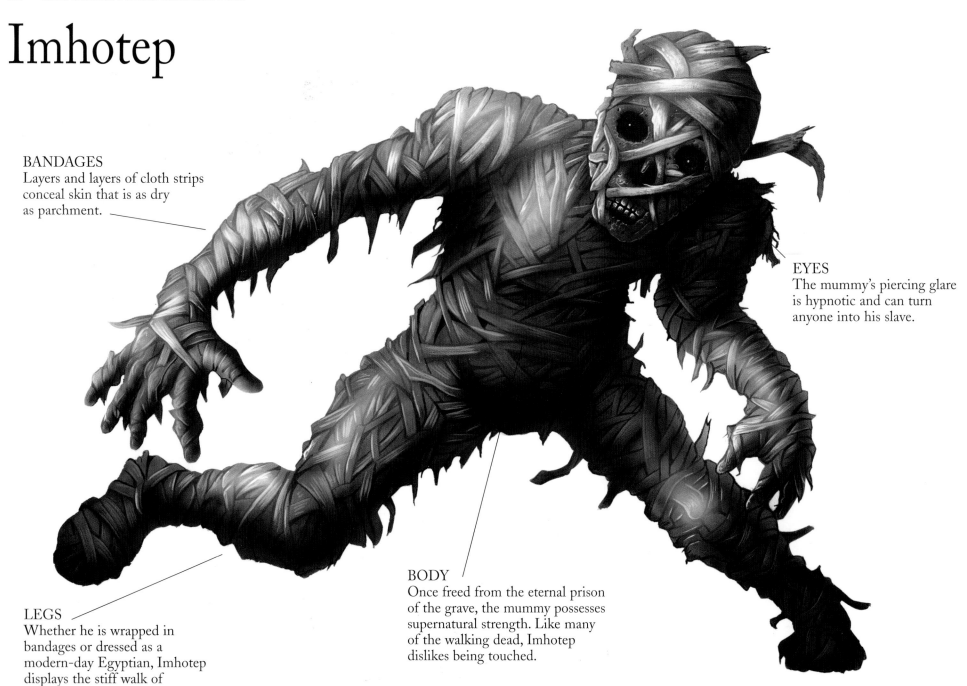

**BANDAGES**
Layers and layers of cloth strips conceal skin that is as dry as parchment.

**EYES**
The mummy's piercing glare is hypnotic and can turn anyone into his slave.

**LEGS**
Whether he is wrapped in bandages or dressed as a modern-day Egyptian, Imhotep displays the stiff walk of the undead.

**BODY**
Once freed from the eternal prison of the grave, the mummy possesses supernatural strength. Like many of the walking dead, Imhotep dislikes being touched.

Imhotep is a priest in ancient Egypt. As punishment for trying to bring his dead princess back to life, he is bandaged like a mummy and buried alive. All sacred symbols and hieroglyphics are removed from his tomb so that his soul will not make the journey to the afterlife. A curse promising insanity and death to anyone who disturbs the mummy is carved in his tomb. More than 3,000 years later, an expedition from the British Museum discovers Imhotep's tomb. The Scroll of Thoth, which contains a spell that can revive the dead, is found in the tomb with the mummy. When the scroll is read aloud, Imhotep comes alive, seizes the scroll, and disappears.

SIZE

▶ IMHOTEP DISGUISES HIMSELF AS A MODERN-DAY EGYPTIAN and approaches archeologists with the location of the princess' tomb. Her tomb is filled with unbelievable riches that are displayed in the Cairo Museum. Imhotep plans to resurrect his princess using the scroll, but a museum security guard interrupts him. The few words he manages to read from the Scroll of Thoth awaken strange feelings in a local woman named Helen. Imhotep begins to pursue Helen, believing she is the reincarnation of his lost love.

## Where in the world?

**Imhotep lay buried in Egypt for 3,700 years before the Scroll of Thoth brought him back to life.**

EGYPT ●

## Did you know?

● Imhotep wishes to use the Scroll of Thoth to transform Helen into his dead princess and make her immortal. When the scroll is burned, Imhotep disintegrates into a crumbled skeleton.

● Because a corpse's eyes and tongue are removed for mummification, a resurrected mummy's first order of business is to snatch eyes and a tongue from a living victim.

● Vladimir Lenin, the Russian revolutionary, is a modern example of a person whose body was preserved by mummification. Lenin's body has been on display in the Lenin Mausoleum in Moscow's Red Square since his death in 1924.

● A mummy was being transported on the RMS *Titanic* when the ship struck an iceberg and sank. Some believe that the mummy's curse caused the disaster at sea.

# Bride of Frankenstein

**FACE**
The dull, black eyes are blank and staring. They dart back and forth in a nervous, birdlike manner. Stitches underneath her chin betray the fact she is the creation of a surgeon.

**HAIR**
The jolt of electricity that brings her to life causes her hair to stand on end and streaks it white.

**HEART**
Her young, fresh heart recently beat in the chest of a peasant girl who was murdered by Frankenstein's assistant.

**BODY**
She has only recently been shocked to life by electricity, so her unnatural movements are twitchy and jerking.

**CLOTHING**
The long tunic is part death shroud, part wedding gown. Bandages still cover her arms like full-length gloves.

Frankenstein's male monster urges the scientist to create a female friend as a mate for him. Frankenstein is reluctant, so the monster kidnaps Frankenstein's fiancée, Elizabeth, and hides her in a cave. The monster blackmails Frankenstein into creating a woman for him, telling him Elizabeth shall be safely returned once he gets his own mate. Using the corpse (stolen from a graveyard) of a 19-year-old girl, Frankenstein goes to work. His assistant is told to get a heart from a victim at the hospital, but instead he murders a peasant girl and takes hers. The female monster is brought to life in the lab during a violent electrical storm.

SIZE

▶ THE STRIKE OF A LIGHTNING BOLT gives the female monster a spark of life. The male creature is hopeful about his new mate and reaches out to touch her arm. She responds to him with an ear-splitting shriek. The male monster is devastated by her rejection. The shortest-lived monster of all time, she survives for only a few minutes before being destroyed. The male monster announces, "We belong dead." He pulls a lever that destroys the lab, himself, and his grotesque, would-be mate.

## Where in the world?

**Frankenstein is up to his old tricks of creating new life from the spare parts of the dead in his secret lab near Geneva, Switzerland.**

GENEVA

## Did you know?

• Frankenstein's first name is Victor in the novel *Frankenstein,* but it is changed to Henry in the movies *Frankenstein* and *Bride of Frankenstein.* The movie version of *Frankenstein* offers a different ending than in the novel. Frankenstein himself survives and his monster is trapped inside a burning mill at the end of the 1931 movie version.

• The bride of Frankenstein actually refers to Elizabeth, Henry Frankenstein's fiancée. While the female monster Frankenstein creates is meant to be a mate for the male monster, she does not survive long enough to be his bride.

# The Blob

BODY
The Blob's body is its only feature. An alien life form in the shape of red jelly, it uses its otherworldly instincts to sense the location of its prey. Its ability to expand is infinite. As long as there are victims to consume, the Blob will continue to grow.

A meteorite lands in a quiet American town. A red gel seeps out of a crack in the meteorite and proceeds to wreak havoc. This alien Blob is an indestructible, ravenous, blood-colored mass that engulfs and dissolves its victims. It grows larger with each victim it consumes. Though physically similar to gelatin, it is a living creature—and one without a conscience. Its only motivation is to consume living flesh, growing fat on blood. It flows around obstacles and can squeeze under doors, ooze through vents, and seep through small cracks. Bullets, electricity, and fire have no effect on the Blob, and the man-eating goo seems unstoppable.

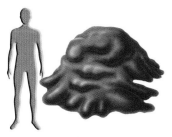

SIZE

▶ AFTER RAMPAGING THROUGH A MOVIE THEATER and chasing the audience into the street, the Blob swallows an entire diner full of panicked patrons. A policeman shoots down electric power lines, which fall on the creature, but they cannot stop the hungry mass. A teenager attempting to put out the fire with an extinguisher discovers that the Blob cannot tolerate cold. Freezing the Blob is the only way to stop it, so fire extinguishers from the school are used to immobilize the Blob in its tracks.

## Where in the world?

● PENNSYLVANIA

**A meteorite lands in the peaceful town of Downingtown, Pennsylvania. Encased within that meteorite is the Blob.**

## Did you know?

● Two teenagers flee the Blob and hide in a cold meat locker at a market. The Blob begins to ooze under the door, but retreats and does not pursue them into the cold.

● To prevent further damage, the frozen Blob is dropped in the Arctic, where it should remain frozen forever.

● *The Blob* was originally released in cinemas in 1958. A sequel entitled *Beware! The Blob* was released in 1972. In the sequel, the Blob is stopped when it is frozen at an ice-skating rink.

● BlobFest is held each year in Phoenixville, Pennsylvania, one of the towns in which *The Blob* was filmed. Activities include a fire extinguisher parade, a scream contest, a re-enactment of the audience fleeing the movie theater, and a competition for the best Blob-themed short film.

# Nosferatu

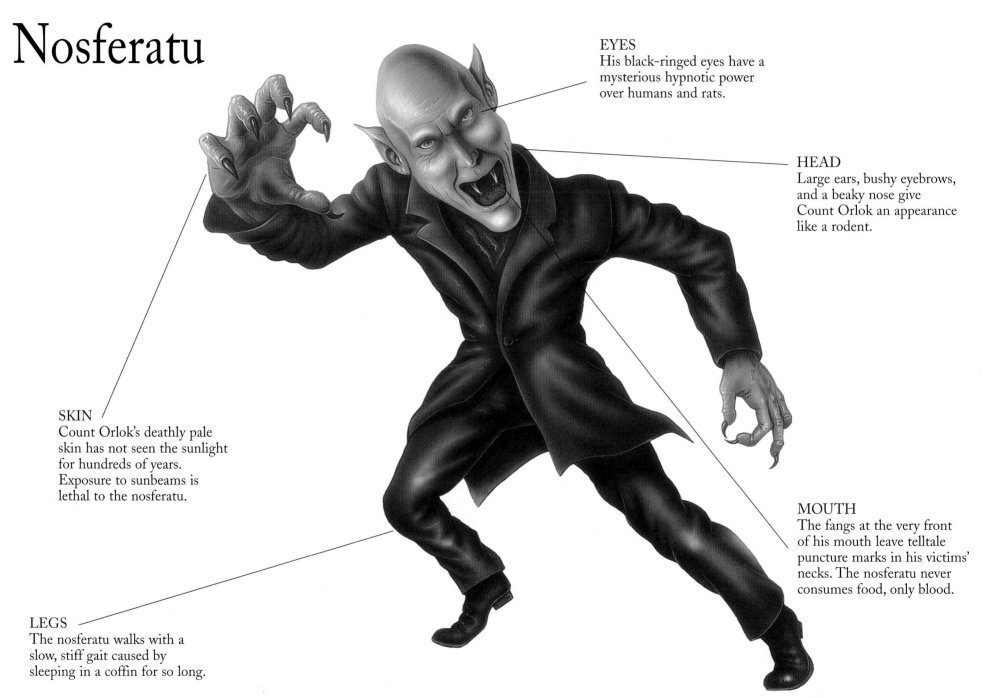

**EYES**
His black-ringed eyes have a mysterious hypnotic power over humans and rats.

**HEAD**
Large ears, bushy eyebrows, and a beaky nose give Count Orlok an appearance like a rodent.

**SKIN**
Count Orlok's deathly pale skin has not seen the sunlight for hundreds of years. Exposure to sunbeams is lethal to the nosferatu.

**MOUTH**
The fangs at the very front of his mouth leave telltale puncture marks in his victims' necks. The nosferatu never consumes food, only blood.

**LEGS**
The nosferatu walks with a slow, stiff gait caused by sleeping in a coffin for so long.

Citizens of Transylvania live in fear of Count Orlok. No coach will dare to transport his visitors to his castle. Orlok is a nosferatu, a ghoul who emerges only at night. He sinks his fangs into the neck of his victim, sucking blood until he is full. His victims all die of the plague. Teetering between life and death, he walks jerkily, like a stiff corpse. Locked doors do not stop him because he has the power to command any door to open. Orlok sails to Germany with coffins containing rats and his native soil. When the ship arrives, the crew is missing. Only the dead captain remains, and his neck bears bizarre puncture wounds.

S I Z E

▶ ORLOK FEEDS ON THE CITIZENS OF GERMANY, spreading plague and leaving mysterious fang marks on their necks. If a woman with a pure heart lures Orlok into the sunlight, he will die. One brave, pure woman invites him into her home. She faints at the sight of the nosferatu and he drinks blood from her neck. Absorbed in savoring his blood feast, Count Orlok forgets about the approaching dawn. Morning light floods in through the window and he disintegrates, turning to smoke.

## Where in the world?

**Count Orlok's castle is located high in Transylvania's Carpathian Mountains. He visits Germany in search of new real estate.**

TRANSYLVANIA

## Did you know?

• Count Orlok tries to suck the blood from a man's cut thumb, but is repelled by the cross the man wears around his neck. By day, Count Orlok sleeps on a layer of Transylvanian soil, sealed in a coffin away from daylight.

• The bite of the nosferatu spreads plague. He does not create new vampires.

• Unlike Count Dracula, Count Orlok casts a shadow and his image can be seen in mirrors.

• Bram Stoker, author of *Dracula,* popularized the word "nosferatu" as an exotic alternative to "vampire."

• The vampire Count Orlok was made famous by F.W. Murnau's 1922 movie *Nosferatu.* Max Schreck, the actor who portrayed Count Orlok in the movie, delivered such a convincing performance that it led to rumors that he was, in fact, a real vampire.

# King Kong

MOUTH
Any human that stands in Kong's way is bitten in half by his large mouth containing sharp teeth.

BODY
Kong's greatest weapon is his size. At 30 feet (9 m) tall, the gorilla destroys a village and also scales the Empire State Building.

ARMS
Brawny arms carry Kong through treetops and give him enough strength to hurl huts through the air and beat a man to death with an uprooted tree.

HANDS
Massive hands are capable of flinging a train from its tracks as if it were a toy, yet Kong can also hold a woman gently in his grasp without crushing her.

A movie crew departs on a secret expedition to the Island of Skull Mountain, planning to film the ancient, monstrous wonder that lives there. The director hires a beautiful, starving actress named Ann, promising her money, adventure, and fame. When the crew reach the island, they witness a hostile tribe worshipping their jungle god, King Kong. A beautiful woman is sacrificed to the huge gorilla, as the tribe drums and chants. Ann is kidnapped and offered as a sacrifice to Kong. Tied to pillars high atop an altar, Ann can only scream helplessly at the sight of Kong. The gorilla beats his chest, bears his teeth, and snarls at Ann.

SIZE

▶ KING KONG PICKS ANN UP IN ONE MIGHTY PAW and carries her off into the depths of the jungle. Numerous prehistoric creatures live within the jungle swamps of the island. Kong battles several dinosaurs to prevent them from eating Ann. The movie crew rescues Ann from Kong as the ape battles a flying pterosaur. Using a gas bomb, the crew captures Kong and transports him back to New York City, where he is put on display. Kong is chained onstage in a Broadway theater so the paying public can gawk at the "Eighth Wonder of the World."

## Where in the world?

**A tribe on the Island of Skull Mountain in the Indian Ocean, just off the western coast of Sumatra, worships the fearsome giant, King Kong.**

INDIAN OCEAN

## Did you know?

● Photographers' flashbulbs startle the chained giant, and Kong breaks his chains and escapes into the streets of New York. He destroys an elevated train before he carries Ann to the top of the Empire State Building. Airplanes open fire at Kong, and while he is able to knock one plane from the sky, the bullets are eventually too much for even the ferocious King Kong. The colossal beast falls to the street below, plummeting 102 stories to his death.

● The original 1933 version of *King Kong* was so popular that a sequel entitled *Son of Kong* was released the same year.

# Jaws

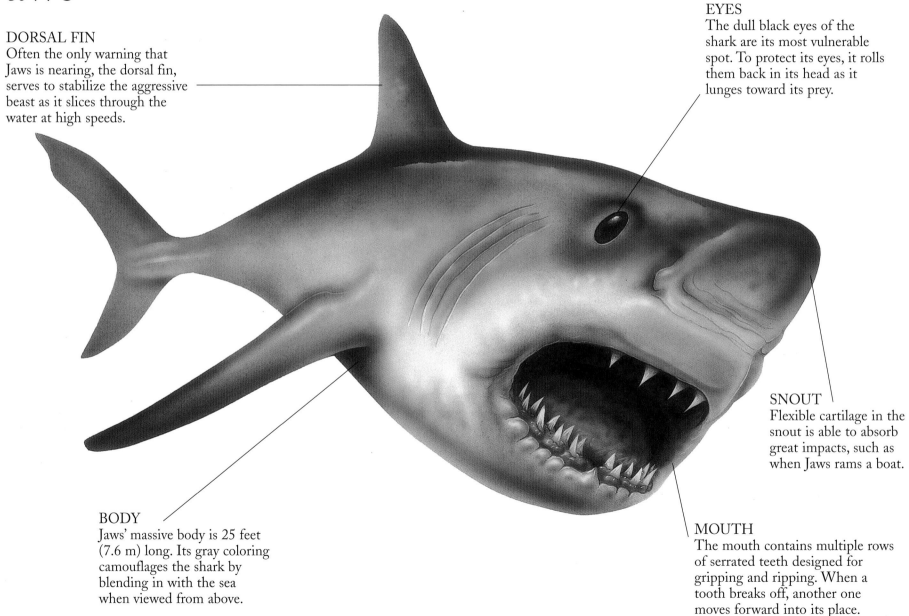

**DORSAL FIN**
Often the only warning that Jaws is nearing, the dorsal fin, serves to stabilize the aggressive beast as it slices through the water at high speeds.

**EYES**
The dull black eyes of the shark are its most vulnerable spot. To protect its eyes, it rolls them back in its head as it lunges toward its prey.

**SNOUT**
Flexible cartilage in the snout is able to absorb great impacts, such as when Jaws rams a boat.

**BODY**
Jaws' massive body is 25 feet (7.6 m) long. Its gray coloring camouflages the shark by blending in with the sea when viewed from above.

**MOUTH**
The mouth contains multiple rows of serrated teeth designed for gripping and ripping. When a tooth breaks off, another one moves forward into its place.

Vacationers at the beach have no idea that just off the shore in the shallows, Jaws is looking for prey. A single fin knifing through the waves may be seen just before the shark strikes. Other times, the shark ambushes its prey from below. Its jaws can easily rip off a human limb or crunch through a torso. The shark sinks its multiple rows of teeth into the victim, and then, shaking its head violently from side to side, it tears through the flesh. A victim may have time to scream—but too late. The water reddens with blood and death is certain.

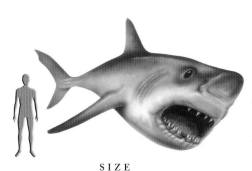

SIZE

▶ IN THE COLD, MURKY DEPTHS OF THE OCEAN, the stealthy shark seeks divers. Jaws rips off a leg of its prey so the diver cannot escape. Shock and blood loss would kill the diver if the hungry shark did not tear him to pieces first. Jaws rams the hulls of boats and heaves its huge body onto the deck of a boat to capsize it. Once the crew is in the water, the merciless animal attacks.

## Where in the world?

**Jaws lurks in the chilly waters of the Atlantic Ocean near Amity Island off of Long Island, New York.**

AMITY ISLAND

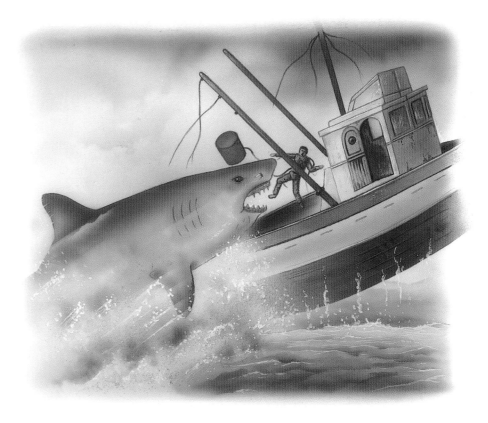

## Did you know?

● The great white shark is found in coastal surface waters and all major oceans of the world.

● A Japanese submarine sank the U.S. Navy ship *Indianapolis* in 1945. Because the ship was on a secret mission, its location was unknown and it took four days for the crew to be rescued. In those four days, sharks devoured 300 crew stranded in the water, helplessly clinging to flotsam as they awaited help.

# Flying Monkeys

**TAIL**
The long tail grasps branches, enabling the monkey to hang from trees in the Haunted Forest.

**WINGS**
Leathery wings like a bat's are thinner than those of birds. This enables the monkey to fly faster and make sharper turns than a bird can.

**HANDS**
Its five-fingered hands enable the monkey to grab girls and dogs.

**LEGS**
Powerful legs can grip their victims while flying with them back to their lair.

**ARMS**
Long, wiry arms enable the monkey to swing from tree to tree in the Haunted Forest and clamber over jagged rocks.

In the Land of Oz, there is a stone castle high atop a craggy mountain. This is the home of the Wicked Witch of the West and her evil flying monkeys. The monkeys obey only the witch, who controls them with her magic hat. The flock of monkeys darken the skies above the countryside outside of Oz's Emerald City. The grinning, hairy creatures are agile and scramble easily over any object in their path. Their great strength enables them to carry heavy loads for long distances while flying. The flying monkey troop makes a terrible sound when assembled, whooping at a volume that can be heard in every corner of the Land of Oz.

SIZE

▶ THE WITCH COMMANDS HER MONKEY SERVANTS TO FLY, and soon the air is thick with the noisy beasts. Their orders are to bring Dorothy and her dog, Toto, back to the witch's castle so that the witch can steal Dorothy's ruby slippers. The flying monkeys rip apart Scarecrow, scattering the stuffing from his legs and chest. They snatch Dorothy and Toto and fly them back to the witch's castle. When Dorothy accidentally kills the witch, the monkeys are freed of the witch's spell and they bow down to Dorothy.

## Where in the world?

The flying monkeys live in the castle belonging to the Wicked Witch of the West, which is located in Winkie Country of the Land of Oz.

**LAND OF OZ**

WINKIE COUNTRY

## Did you know?

● After the monkeys fling Scarecrow's legs and chest in different directions, his friends Tin Man and Cowardly Lion have to restuff him before they can find Dorothy and rescue her from the witch.

● The captain of the flying monkeys is named Nikko.

● Like many other varieties of monkey, the flying monkeys live in a troop of about 30 monkeys and are rarely seen alone.

● Since 1976, sculptures of winged monkeys have watched over the city of Burlington, Vermont, from the top of a historic building.

● Flying monkeys and bats are the only mammals capable of flight.

# Hannibal Lecter

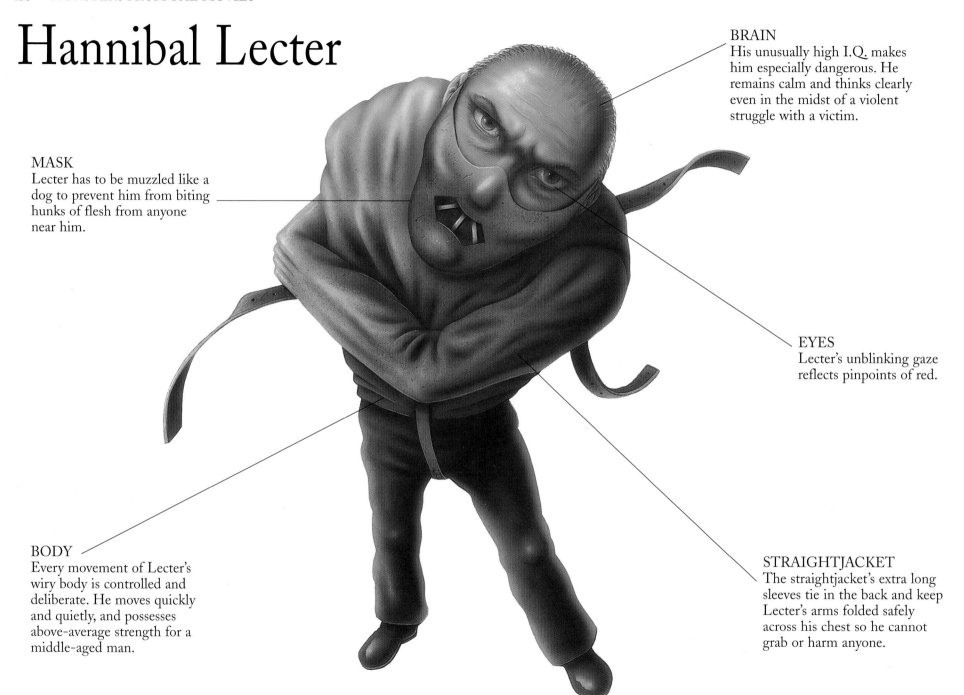

**BRAIN**
His unusually high I.Q. makes him especially dangerous. He remains calm and thinks clearly even in the midst of a violent struggle with a victim.

**MASK**
Lecter has to be muzzled like a dog to prevent him from biting hunks of flesh from anyone near him.

**EYES**
Lecter's unblinking gaze reflects pinpoints of red.

**BODY**
Every movement of Lecter's wiry body is controlled and deliberate. He moves quickly and quietly, and possesses above-average strength for a middle-aged man.

**STRAIGHTJACKET**
The straightjacket's extra long sleeves tie in the back and keep Lecter's arms folded safely across his chest so he cannot grab or harm anyone.

D r. Hannibal "the Cannibal" Lecter is a genius who can boast of being a psychiatrist, count, and culinary artist. However, he is also a torturer, cannibal—and serial killer. Hannibal Lecter was raised at Castle Lecter in Lithuania. As a child during World War II, he witnesses his sister being butchered and eaten. While attending medical school in France, Lecter tracks down and kills the men who slaughtered his sister. He does not kill at random, murdering only those who have offended him. His victims end up as a five-star meal.

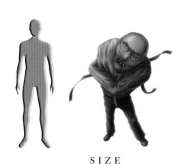

SIZE

► HANNIBAL LECTER FEELS NEITHER PITY nor remorse for any of his crimes. He is so cold-blooded that his pulse does not race while he is committing a murder. Lecter is so malicious and brilliantly persuasive that he talks a fellow inmate into swallowing his own tongue. Rather than simply cooperating and assisting the authorities in their hunt for another serial killer, Lecter turns the hunt into a game for his own amusement. Lecter is eventually able to escape prison by cutting off the face of a guard and using it as a mask.

## Where in the world?

**Hannibal Lecter practices both psychiatry and cannibalism in the greater Baltimore area, in Maryland.**

BALTIMORE

## Did you know?

• One of Hannibal Lecter's favorite recipes involves sautéing the internal organs of his victims in a butter sauce.

• A flute player with the Baltimore Orchestra becomes one of Lecter's victims when his poor playing interferes with the killer's enjoyment of the concerts. Lecter serves up several of the flute player's internal organs at a dinner he holds for the orchestra's board of directors.

• Lecter is featured in a number of Thomas Harris' novels: *Red Dragon*, *The Silence of the Lambs*, *Hannibal*, and *Hannibal Rising*.

# Jason

**VOICE**
Eerily silent, he never utters a word of explanation during any of the chilling murders he commits.

**FACE**
A mask hides Jason's deformed face. On some occasions, he wears a bag over his head to hide his features.

**BODY**
Jason possesses superhuman strength and the strange power to recover from any injury. Machetes, bullets, axes, and toxic waste cannot stop him.

**MACHETE**
Jason employs a variety of methods to kill his victims, but a razor-sharp machete is his weapon of choice.

Jason Voorhees is a silent, unstoppable killer who commits a series of gruesome murders without ever uttering a single word. He lives as a hermit in the woods, emerging only to kill. It is impossible to destroy Jason. He survives a shooting, a stabbing with a machete, a blow to the head with an ax, a burial, an exposure to toxic waste, a boat propeller strike to his face, and three drownings. Just when he is

believed to be dead, he is brought back to life by an underwater electrical cable. On another occasion, his lifeless body is revived after his chest is pierced by an iron fence post that is struck by a bolt of lightning.

SIZE

▶ AS A YOUNGSTER, Jason drowns one summer while swimming at Camp Crystal Lake. His body is never recovered from the lake. Jason's mother, upset at the loss of her only son, avenges his death by murdering the counselors and campers. Serial killing runs in the family, and Jason has a talent for murder. His inventive methods include using an ice pick, a pitchfork, a machete, a spear gun, barbed wire, a fire poker, and a wrench as weapons. He also kills by strangling and slashing throats.

## Where in the world?

**Camp Crystal Lake, where Jason drowned, is located in the northeastern state of New Jersey. The murders there earned it the nickname "Camp Blood."**

CAMP CRYSTAL LAKE

## Did you know?

● Jason kills more than 100 people over the course of 10 days.

● Jason's mother is beheaded by one of the campers she is attempting to kill. The death of his mother awakens in Jason a thirst for revenge, and he grows up alone in the woods without any family. He builds a shrine around his mother's severed head. When the long-closed Camp Crystal Lake is reopened, Jason continues the family tradition of killing and sets out to avenge his mother's death.

● Even though Jason is a fictional character, he was awarded MTV's Lifetime Achievement Award in 1992.

# Zombies

**BRAIN**
Even though its brain is not active, a zombie can only be permanently stopped by destroying its brain.

**NOSE**
With an acute sense of smell, a zombie can detect the odor of human prey up to a mile away.

**MOUTH**
The zombie uses no spoken language, but only moans. It consumes human flesh.

**LIMBS**
Having its limbs cut off does not bother a zombie. It will continue to seek flesh for as long as its brain is intact.

**BODY**
As an undead being, a zombie may reek of the grave or have body parts that are rotting away.

A zombie is an undead corpse that feeds on living human flesh. When a zombie bites a living human, it passes on an infection in the form of a virus. The virus travels through the victim's bloodstream, infecting the brain, and all bodily functions stop. The victim's brain remains alive but inactive. Symptoms resulting from a zombie bite include bruising of the bitten area, fever, slowed heart rate, numbness, and coma. By the next day, the victim rises as a zombie. The zombie spends all of its time in search of a new victim. Despite its slow shuffle, the zombie is an efficient killer and can live for several years before it rots completely away.

SIZE

▶ THE ONLY WAY TO KILL A ZOMBIE is by destroying its brain. Blunt objects, axes, guns, harpoons, crossbows, and chainsaws have all proven to be effective weapons for destroying the zombie's brain. However, it is unwise to engage a zombie in hand-to-hand combat. Protective gear, such as armor or a mesh shark suit, should be worn when approaching a zombie, to guard against its lethal bite. Zombies cannot be burned to death, and a burning zombie produces an incredible stink.

## Where in the world?

**Zombies roam the entire Earth, turning the living into flesh-eating undead with their bites.**

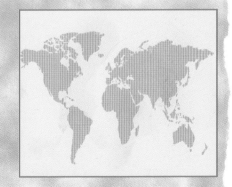

## Did you know?

● Zombies tend to gather in cities. In the event of a zombie outbreak, avoid urban areas.

● Any person bitten by a zombie should be shot in the head. Even though they appear to be dead, a day later the victim will rise as a member of the living dead.

● The belief that a voodoo priest can change a person into a zombie has persisted for generations in Haiti.

● In the 1968 movie *Night of the Living Dead*, which is considered to be on influential zombie movies of all time, the word "zombie" is never used. The are referred to as "those things."

# Frankenstein's Monster

**EYES**
His glowing, yellowed eyes deliver a fixed stare that chills anyone who dares to look directly at him.

**BRAIN**
Even though his brain was once dead, the monster is intelligent. He is able to speak, read, and show complex emotions.

**SKIN**
The creature's yellow skin is so thin that his muscles and blood vessels are nearly visible.

**BODY**
His body is fashioned out of cold parts from bodies snatched out of graves. The monster stands 8 feet (2.4 m) tall and possesses incredible strength.

Pieced together from body parts stolen from graves, Frankenstein's monster is a terrible reminder that Man should not attempt to play God. Victor Frankenstein believes that electricity can be used as a power source to bring the dead back to life. He harnesses powers meant only for God, and the result is that he creates a monster which destroys him. Frankenstein conducts a series of experiments on stolen corpses. When a bolt of lightning brings his monster to life in the lab, Frankenstein is immediately sorry. He intended his creation to be beautiful, but it is revolting. Horrified, Frankenstein runs away from his awful creation.

SIZE

▶ FRANKENSTEIN AWAKES TO SEE THE GHASTLY MONSTER standing at his bedside. Once again, he flees his creation. When Frankenstein's brother is murdered, the monster admits killing him as a way to strike back at his creator for rejecting him. The lonely monster begs Frankenstein to create a mate for him. Frankenstein begins work on a female creature, but his conscience forces him to destroy her and dump her lifeless body in a lake. As revenge, the furious monster murders Frankenstein's bride on their wedding night.

## Where in the world?

**The secret lab where Victor Frankenstein brings his monster to life is in an unknown location near Geneva, Switzerland.**

GENEVA

## Did you know?

• Frankenstein spends the rest of his life pursuing the monster to take revenge for the death of his bride. He tracks the creature to the icy Arctic and chases him on a dogsled, but the ice between them separates in a huge crack. When Frankenstein dies, the monster weeps over the body of his creator. The creature heads off across the ice to die alone.

• Mary Shelley wrote the novel *Frankenstein* when she was 19 years old.

• The name "Frankenstein" is often incorrectly used to refer to Victor Frankenstein's creation. Throughout the book, his creation is referred to as "the creature" or "the monster." Frankenstein is the name of the scientist who created the monster.

# Dracula

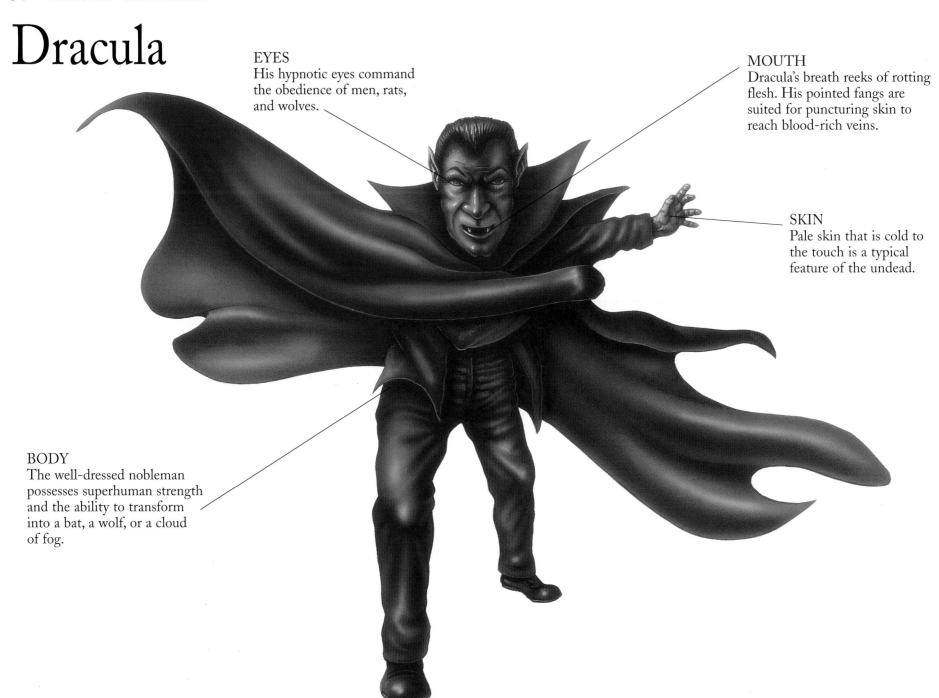

EYES
His hypnotic eyes command the obedience of men, rats, and wolves.

MOUTH
Dracula's breath reeks of rotting flesh. His pointed fangs are suited for puncturing skin to reach blood-rich veins.

SKIN
Pale skin that is cold to the touch is a typical feature of the undead.

BODY
The well-dressed nobleman possesses superhuman strength and the ability to transform into a bat, a wolf, or a cloud of fog.

Count Dracula, the most famous vampire in history, must drink human blood in order to survive. If he does not drink blood regularly, he will begin to age rapidly. Although hundreds of years old, Dracula maintains the appearance of a wealthy middle-aged nobleman thanks to his diet of blood. Elisabeta is the love of his life, and when she dies, Dracula rejects God and curses the living. The count uses black magic to rise from the grave as a vampire. The only companions in his grim, remote castle are his three undead vampire brides. Dracula decides it is time for him to expand his territory and he hires a real estate agent.

SIZE

▶ DRACULA SETS SAIL FOR LONDON, taking with him coffins containing his native soil. The vampire discovers that Mina, the fiancée of his real estate agent, resembles his long-dead love Elisabeta. Dracula appears in Mina's bedroom at night. He plans to transform her into a vampire with his bite and by feeding her his own blood. Once she is a vampire, Mina will be doomed to drink blood or die. Before she can be fully transformed, Dracula is hunted down. His throat is slashed and he is stabbed through the heart with a knife.

## Where in the world?

TRANSYLVANIA

**Dracula's secluded castle is located in the Carpathian Mountains of Transylvania, which is part of modern-day Romania.**

## Did you know?

• When Dracula is killed, the bite marks on Mina's neck disappear and she is free of the vampire's curse.

• The preferred method of killing a vampire is to drive a wooden stake through its heart and decapitate it to prevent it from returning to life.

• A creature of the night, Dracula is less powerful during the hours of daylight. His otherworldly nature means that the vampire does not cast a shadow and mirrors do not show his reflection.

• Bram Stoker, the author of *Dracula,* was a sickly child. He was bedridden for the first seven years of his life. His mother told him horror stories to entertain him. When he was finally well enough to leave the house, his playground was the local graveyard.

# The Headless Horseman

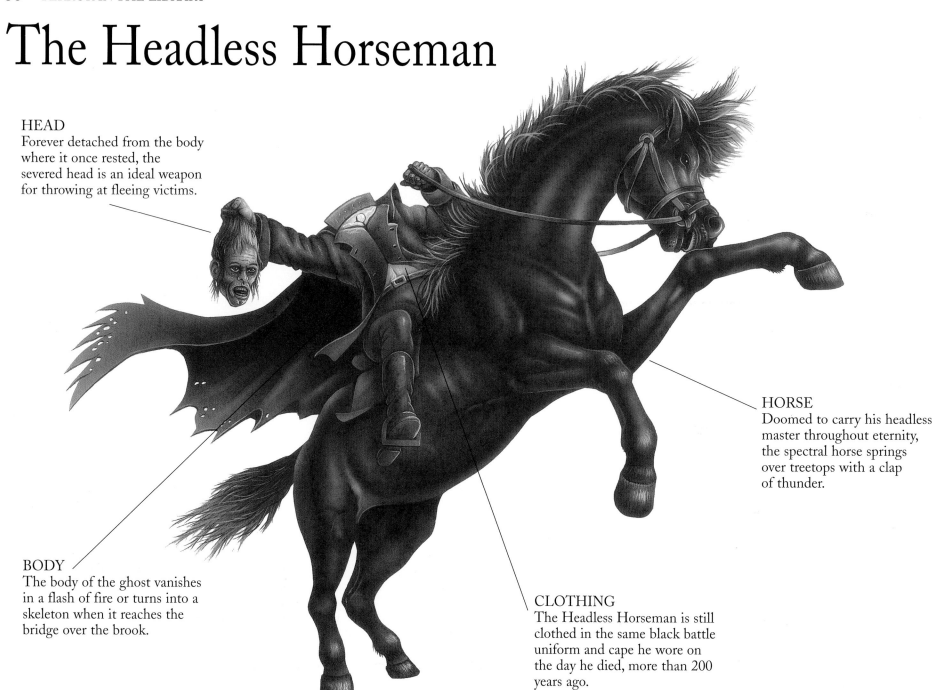

**HEAD**
Forever detached from the body where it once rested, the severed head is an ideal weapon for throwing at fleeing victims.

**BODY**
The body of the ghost vanishes in a flash of fire or turns into a skeleton when it reaches the bridge over the brook.

**CLOTHING**
The Headless Horseman is still clothed in the same black battle uniform and cape he wore on the day he died, more than 200 years ago.

**HORSE**
Doomed to carry his headless master throughout eternity, the spectral horse springs over treetops with a clap of thunder.

The ghost of a soldier who was beheaded by a cannonball during the American Revolutionary War haunts the town of Sleepy Hollow. Every night, the spirit rides his black horse to the scene of the battle in search of his missing head. In the early hours of the morning, the drowsy townsfolk hear the horse galloping to return the soldier to his grave in the churchyard before dawn. Riding home one night, Ichabod Crane, the local schoolmaster, hears the sound of horse's hooves behind him. Crane twists around in his saddle to see the horrible specter of the Headless Horseman.

SIZE

▶ SITTING SILENTLY ON HIS HORSE, with his detached head resting on his saddle, is the dead soldier. Crane spurs his horse frantically to escape, but the Headless Horseman chases him. Crane hurries his horse toward the brook by the church, knowing that he will be safe once he crosses the bridge. After he crosses the bridge, Crane turns to look at the ghost. The Headless Horseman rises in his stirrups and throws his severed head at Crane. The head strikes Crane and knocks him from his horse.

## Where in the world?

SLEEPY HOLLOW

**For more than two centuries, the Headless Horseman has ridden through the small town of Sleepy Hollow near the Hudson River in New York State.**

## Did you know?

• Ichabod Crane disappears from Sleepy Hollow after his ride at midnight with the Headless Horseman. His cap is found near the church and his horse is found near his home, but the schoolmaster is never seen in the town again.

• The entire town of Sleepy Hollow is under an old spell that causes inhabitants to hear music and voices in the air, see strange sights, and fall into trances. The townsfolk are superstitious and can point out any number of haunted spots to the visitor.

• Ghosts cannot cross running water, which is why Ichabod Crane is safe from the Headless Horseman once he crosses the bridge over the brook.

• All ghosts must return to their graves before dawn.

# Triffid

STINGER
The stinger, which is similar to a tongue, rapidly lashes out at prey, aiming for the face or head of its victim. The venom acts immediately, blinding or killing a man within seconds of the sting.

HEAD
Hollow and brightly colored, the flowerlike head contains both the stinger and a sticky substance used by the Triffid to trap insects.

STEM
Its stalk carries nutrients from the roots to the head of the Triffid.

BASE
A mass of roots consisting of thick tentacles can anchor the Triffid into the ground or move it along the ground at a walking speed.

Triffid seeds stolen from a Soviet research lab are caught in the winds and scattered across the earth. They take root. The plant has a lethal stinger, but is not considered dangerous. Collectors remove the stingers and cultivate the plants in greenhouses. Scientists discover that Triffids can be grown as a commercial crop because of their valuable oils and protein. However, as the plants multiply, the peril increases. Triffids can uproot themselves and move about at will. Each plant emits a slow, clicking sound that grows faster and faster as it zeroes in on a target.

SIZE

▶ THE POISONOUS STINGER WHIPS OUT OF THE TRIFFID'S HEAD and strikes its victim, leaving behind dark green venom and a painful welt with cuts. The Triffid roots itself next to a fallen victim and waits for the flesh to decay. Rotted flesh is easier for the stinger to pull inside its head and absorb. When an intense burst of light from a meteor shower blinds most people on Earth, Triffids easily pick off the sightless humans. As the Triffids take over, city dwellers are forced to move to the countryside to escape the threat.

## Where in the world?

SOVIET UNION

**Triffid seeds are scattered across the earth when the airplane carrying them is destroyed in flight. They were originally stolen from a Soviet laboratory.**

## Did you know?

- The most effective way to kill a Triffid is by severing its trunk or destroying its head bud. Because it has no internal organs, it cannot be killed with bullets. Burning a Triffid is a less effective method for destroying it because of the possibility of the flames causing other fires.

- Some people believe that dousing a Triffid with saltwater is the best way to stop the hostile vegetation in its tracks.

- A Triffid's stinger will grow back when damaged.

- Although Triffids move slowly, they are able to climb stairs and shove obstacles out of their way while searching for victims.

- John Wyndham created the deadly plants in his 1951 novel, *The Day of the Triffids*.

# Morlocks

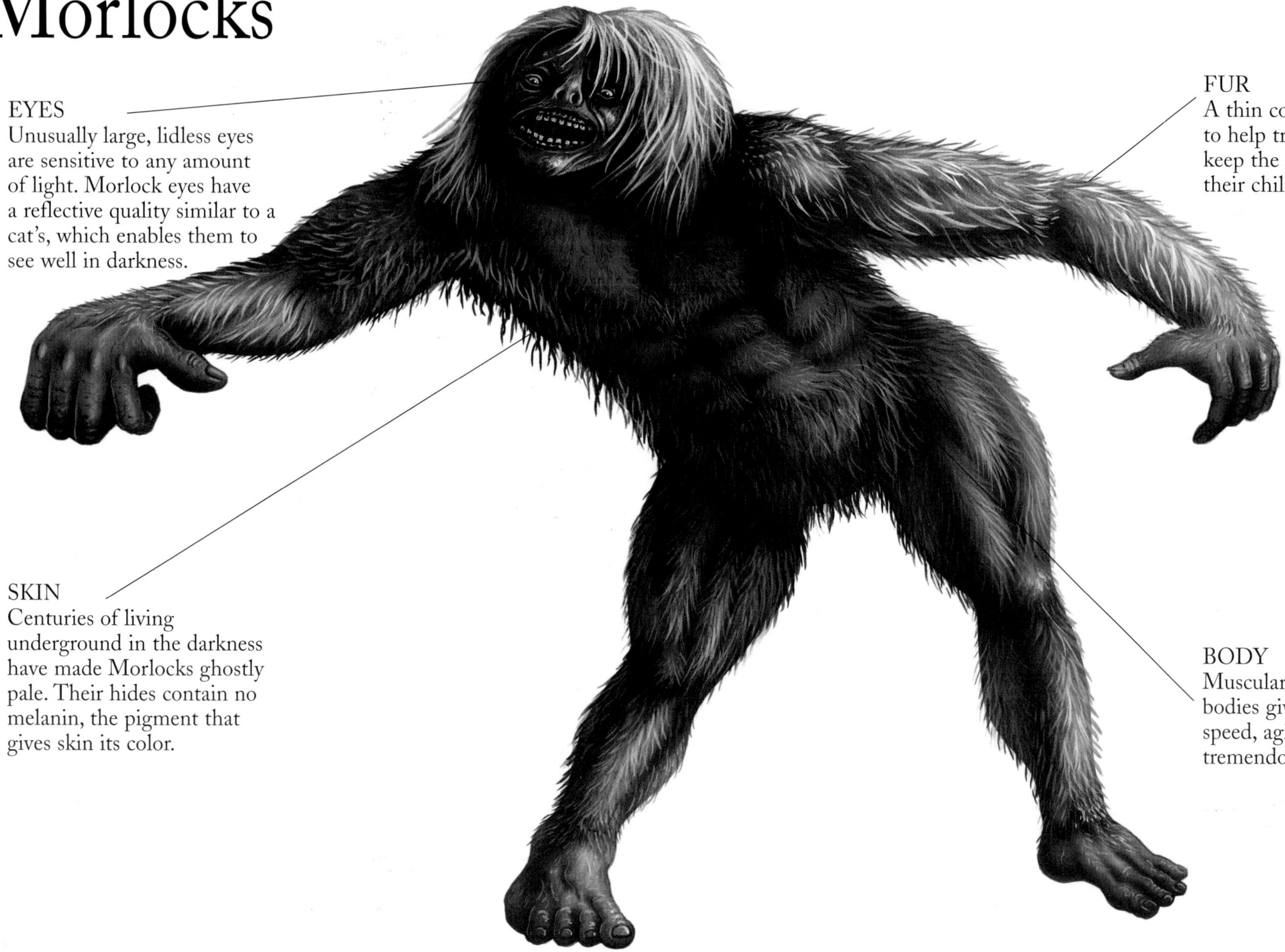

**EYES**
Unusually large, lidless eyes
are sensitive to any amount
of light. Morlock eyes have
a reflective quality similar to a
cat's, which enables them to
see well in darkness.

**FUR**
A thin coat of fur is essential
to help trap body heat and
keep the Morlocks warm in
their chilly burrows.

**SKIN**
Centuries of living
underground in the darkness
have made Morlocks ghostly
pale. Their hides contain no
melanin, the pigment that
gives skin its color.

**BODY**
Muscular, apelike
bodies give the Morlock
speed, agility, and
tremendous strength.

Deep beneath the surface of Earth dwells an apelike race called *Morlocks*. These pale, fur-covered creatures live in the darkness below England in the year A.D. 802,701. The Morlocks tend ancient machines in their black caverns. Both their fur and lair smell foul, and reek of the blood of their victims. Their large, reflective eyes are so accustomed to the darkness underground that they are blinded by any amount of light, and even the glow from a match is painful to them. Morlocks emerge from their world only at night, to snatch surface dwellers and drag them back to their caverns to feast on their flesh.

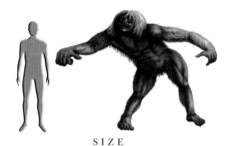

SIZE

▶ MORLOCKS FEED ON THE LAZY, passive surface dwellers called *Eloi*. Morlocks treat the Eloi like livestock, providing them with food and shelter until the time comes to haul them away to be killed and eaten underground. The entrances to the Morlock world are a series of structures that resemble circular wells. These entrances are spread across the countryside, giving the Morlocks easy access to the Eloi. The steady sound of thudding machinery far below the ground can be heard at the mouths of these wells.

## Where in the world?

**By the 8,028th century, according to H.G. Wells' novella *The Time Machine*, Morlocks had adapted to living in their subterranean lair beneath England.**

● ENGLAND

## Did you know?

● Both the Eloi and Morlock races are descended from the human race. The Eloi more closely resemble humans, but they are a weak, childlike race that lounges around all day, doing no work.

● A time traveler discovers the Morlocks. He begins his journey in London during the year 1895 and travels forward to the 8,028th century, thinking that life on Earth will be better in the future.

● The time machine is stolen by the Morlocks. The time traveler has to battle the Morlocks to retrieve his machine. Barely escaping being ripped to shreds by the Morlocks, he races even further forward in time to escape them.

# Jabberwock

**WINGS**
Its batlike wings are not powerful enough to lift the heavy beast from the ground. The Jabberwock flaps his wings while attacking to terrify its prey.

**EYES**
Its bulging, red eyes of flame reflect the Jabberwock's demonic nature.

**CLAWS**
Sharp, bony claws catch and scratch with such a fury that all the flesh is raked from its victim's body.

**MOUTH**
Its gaping jaws are lined with sharp fangs. The Jabberwock emits a terrifying bleating noise before it chomps down on its victim.

An engine of mindless destruction, the Jabberwock turns a peaceful British forest into a killing ground. The towering Jabberwock parts the trees, flattening brush beneath its clawed feet. The tranquil sound of chirping birds is silenced by the shrieks of the Jabberwock's victim. The monster strips its prey of flesh and innards, leaving behind only bloodied bones. It ravages the countryside, eating livestock and people, and flattening villages. Anyone wandering into the forest to gather firewood or trap a rabbit for dinner runs the risk of being eaten. The population is terrified. Many people living in the countryside flee to the city for protection.

SIZE

▶ ONE DAY, A BRAVE MAN MARCHES ALONE INTO THE DARK WOOD with his vorpal sword in search of the Jabberwock. He intends to free the kingdom of the hideous menace. He rests beside a tree, lost in thought, when he hears the Jabberwock rumbling through the woods toward him. He runs his sword through the monster's scaly body. When the sword pierces its body, the Jabberwock screeches and oozes green blood. It collapses dead on the forest floor. The thud of its falling body can be heard throughout the woods.

## Where in the world?

**According to Lewis Carroll's** *Through the Looking-Glass and What Alice Found There,* **the Jabberwock inhabits a dense wood in England.**

● ENGLAND

## Did you know?

● The man who slays the Jabberwock returns triumphantly to the city, carrying the beast's severed head to show everyone that the forest is safe again.

● John Tenniel's original illustration of the Jabberwock depicts the beast wearing a vest over its scaly body. The image was supposed to serve as the first illustration in the book, but the author thought it might frighten children and had it placed within the text.

● For the 1977 movie *Jabberwocky,* the Jabberwock was advertised as "the monster so horrible that people caught the plague to avoid it" and "the monster the monsters are frightened of."

# Mr. Hyde

**FACE**
An unpleasant smile reflects Hyde's rotten soul. His face is not disfigured, but to anyone who looks at him, he appears wicked and disagreeable.

**BODY**
His pale, squat body and offensive manner make Hyde the sort of person no one wants to look at for long.

**CLOTHING**
He wears the clothing of a gentleman, but Hyde is a rough and repulsive man. His garments are loose because his stunted body cannot fill the well-proportioned clothes of a gentleman.

**HANDS**
Hyde kills a man by beating him to death for no reason other than it amuses him to do so.

Friends of the respectable Dr. Jekyll begin to worry when a disgusting man named Mr. Hyde is seen going in and out of the doctor's house. Dr. Jekyll is a handsome, well-mannered man, and his friends fear that Mr. Hyde will take advantage of Dr. Jekyll's wealth. Word spreads that Hyde trampled a young girl in the street one night and showed no remorse. Hyde's violence worsens when he encounters a respected member of the government one evening. For no reason, Hyde clubs him to death with a heavy cane, then tramples him underfoot. Hyde is obviously a lunatic, and Jekyll's friends think the doctor should be warned.

SIZE

▶ IN TRUTH, Dr. Jekyll has been secretly conducting experiments in his lab. When he drinks a potion he has invented, the good Dr. Jekyll transforms into the hideous Mr. Hyde. Hyde embodies all the worst qualities in human nature. He takes nightly trips to the darker side of town, where he menaces the population and engages in illegal activities. The violent Hyde grows stronger than Dr. Jekyll, and the doctor has trouble keeping the dangerous Hyde under control. Jekyll commits suicide to kill the evil Mr. Hyde.

## Where in the world?

**Mr. Hyde can be found prowling the dark back streets of London, England, in pursuit of a lawless evening.**

● LONDON

## Did you know?

● Dr. Jekyll meant for his potion to separate the good from the evil in a person. Instead, it led to his own darker side taking over his personality.

● The truth about Dr. Jekyll and Mr. Hyde being two sides of the same person is not known until a letter containing Dr. Jekyll's confession is read after his death.

● Robert Louis Stevenson based *The Strange Case of Dr. Jekyll and Mr. Hyde* on a real-life Scottish businessman named Deacon Brodie, who led a double life. Brodie was an upstanding citizen by day, but a thief, burglar, and gambler by night. Brodie was captured during an attempted robbery in 1786 and was hanged for his crimes.

# Orc

**BODY**
His short, deformed body is filthy. The Orc's long arms, crooked back, and bowed legs give him an apelike appearance.

**FACE**
The Orc's piggy face is flat-nosed with sallow skin and beady, slanted eyes.

**MOUTH**
The fanged mouth never smiles. It produces an unpleasant laugh that sounds like clashing metal.

**WEAPONS**
An Orc will choose a rock, a club, or poisoned blades and arrows as battle weapons.

Orcs are sadistic, warmongering beings capable only of destruction. They create nothing but misery and conflict. Orcs are wretched creatures. They hate everyone, including their own race. Their hearts of granite pump sour black blood through their veins. Orcs are always hungry and consume the flesh of humans and horses alike. Frodo the hobbit is lucky to survive being captured by Orcs after the demon spider Shelob paralyzes him. The Orcs discover the unconscious Frodo wrapped in the spider's webbing. Frodo is carried away to the Orcs' lair, but his friend Sam rescues him before the Orcs can make a meal of him.

SIZE

► EVIL LORD SAURON BREEDS AND USES THE ORCS as his foot soldiers in wars against the Elves and Men. Called the Foot Soldiers of Shadow, the Orcs are bred for great size, speed, and malice. Orcs wear thick, black armor etched with spells and a helmet bearing the horns of a Mûmak, a mammoth ancestor of modern-day elephants. Orcs make the fiercest of warriors because they are willing to take on any enemy. When no enemy is available, Orcs frequently fight among themselves.

## Where in the world?

**The Orcs' home base is Mordor, but they range throughout Middle-earth, engaging in battle with hobbits, Men, Dwarves, and Elves alike.**

MIDDLE-EARTH

MORDOR

## Did you know?

● In Tolkien's fantasy novel *The Lord of the Rings*, a group of Orcs invades the land where the hobbits live. A battle breaks out between the hobbits and the Orc invaders. One of the hobbits uses a club to knock the head off of the chief Orc. The Orc's severed head flies through the air and lands in a rabbit hole. According to the hobbits, this hole-in-one led to the invention of golf.

● While Frodo is held in the Orcs' lair, the Orcs search through his belongings in search of the One Ring. The Orcs become involved in a dispute over who will take Frodo's metal vest. The dispute grows into a battle between all the Orcs present, and nearly all of them are killed in the argument over ownership of the vest.

# Shelob

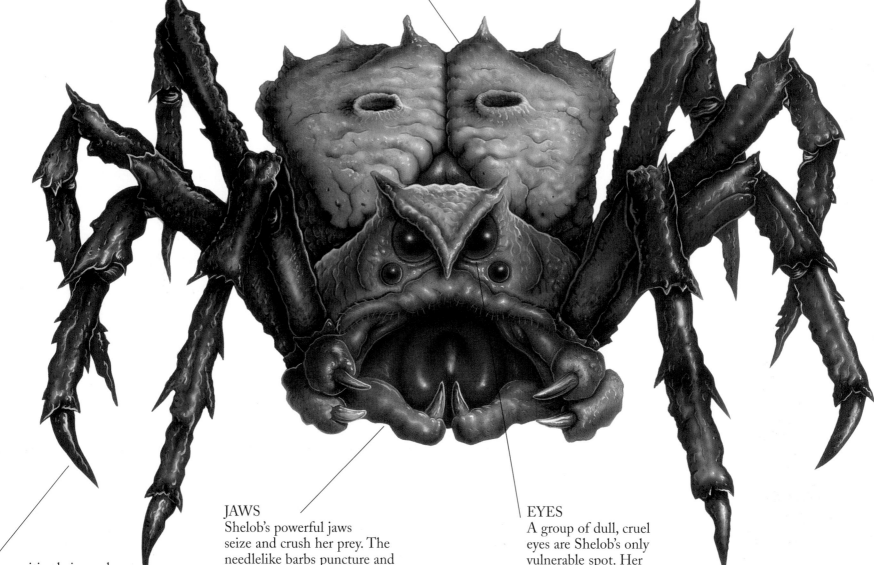

**SKIN**
Her bumpy, pitted hide is
so thick that no weapon
can pierce it.

**LEGS**
The ultra-sensitive hairs on her
legs detect movement and the
scent of her prey approaching.

**JAWS**
Shelob's powerful jaws
seize and crush her prey. The
needlelike barbs puncture and
inject poison into her victim.

**EYES**
A group of dull, cruel
eyes are Shelob's only
vulnerable spot. Her
natural habitat is darkness,
so any amount of light is
painful to her.

A demon in spider form, Shelob lives in a dark, foul-smelling lair of underground tunnels, and devours any living thing that approaches along Spider's Pass. The evil Lord Sauron uses Shelob to guard one of the entrances to his realm. Sauron throws her an Orc every few days to keep her happy. She spins ropelike webs that even a sword cannot break. Somewhere in the maze of black, reeking tunnels she waits, the sensitive hairs on her legs detecting the approach of her next meal. When a victim is tangled in her web, she uses her stinger and needlelike jaws to pump a paralyzing poison into his veins.

SIZE

▶ SHELOB IS FAT FROM DRINKING THE BLOOD OF MEN, Orcs, and Elves. She attacks and stings the hobbit Frodo in the neck, leaving him paralyzed and helpless. Frodo's friend Sam rips off one of Shelob's legs and puts out one of her eyes, which are the only soft spots on her body. In a fury, she tries to crush Sam beneath her massive body, but she is impaled on Frodo's sword. The injury is not enough to kill her, but she scurries away, wounded.

## Where in the world?

MIDDLE-EARTH

MORDOR

Shelob awaits her next victim in the dark caverns located high in Middle-earth's mountains of Mordor, according to J.R.R. Tolkien's *The Two Towers*.

## Did you know?

• Frodo attempts to slash Shelob with his sword before she is able to attack him, but her armored skin cannot be cut open.

• Frodo lights the way through Shelob's lair using the Star-glass, which contains a fragment of the Evening Star's light. Shelob is accustomed to complete darkness, so the light from the Star-glass is painful to her eyes.

• Frodo and Sam are led into Spider's Pass by Gollum, a servant of Shelob. Gollum intends to steal the One Ring from Frodo after Shelob devours Frodo and Sam.

• Shelob's webs are as strong as steel. She wraps her paralyzed victims in the silk she spins, and leaves them until she is ready to dine on their blood.

# Lord Sauron

**HALBERD**
Sauron swings a halberd, a pike with a double-bladed ax, against enemies on horseback in battle.

**HANDS**
His hands burn like fire to the touch.

**ARMOR**
On the battlefield, Sauron wears a suit of plate armor spiked with demonic horns.

**SWORD**
A talented ironsmith, Sauron carries a sword he forged himself.

**BODY**
Sauron is a shape-shifter, who appears as a handsome man, a werewolf, a dark shadow, or a black knight. Though not a giant, Sauron does stand taller than other men.

Sauron is a dark lord with the ability to change his appearance at will. He can take the shape of a handsome man or change into a werewolf or dark shadow. Sauron's servants are werewolves and vampires. He wages war against the Elves, and when he conquers their island, he turns it into the Isle of Werewolves. After Sauron's evil master is defeated during the War of Wrath, Sauron goes into hiding for about 1,000 years. He reappears in the form of an attractive man and seems to have changed his ways, but his true plan is to seize power over all men. He convinces the Elves to forge the nine Rings of Power, which give incredible power to their owners.

SIZE

▶ SAURON SECRETLY FORGES THE ONE RING, which controls the other nine rings. He erects the Dark Tower and becomes known as Dark Lord of Mordor. His body is struck down in battle and the finger with the One Ring is cut off. Even when his body is destroyed, his spirit lives on as an enormous yellow eye ringed with fire. The unblinking, lidless eye hangs over the Dark Tower. Sauron's power is destroyed with the destruction of the One Ring in the fires of Mount Doom.

## Where in the world?

MORDOR

**The fiery, yellow eye of Lord Sauron hangs above the Dark Tower, keeping watch over all of Middle-earth in J.R.R. Tolkien's** *The Lord of the Rings.*

## Did you know?

- Lord Sauron can live only as long as the One Ring exists because he has invested so much of his own power in the ring. When the One Ring is destroyed, Sauron's spirit rises as a black cloud, but a west wind blows the evil cloud away and the Dark Tower crumbles.

- Sauron controls all of the Orcs in Middle-earth. He breeds Orcs to use as soldiers and as servants.

- The nine Rings of Power are given to human kings who fall under the power of Sauron and his One Ring. The kings are transformed into Ringwraiths.

- The only way to destroy the One Ring is to throw it into the fires of Mount Doom, where Sauron originally forged it.

# Ringwraith

**SWORD**
He is armed with a steel sword, but his greatest weapon is the terror that radiates from the Ringwraith.

**EYES**
Only a faint reflection remains where his eyes once were.

**BODY**
His body has faded away, making him invisible to mortals, but the Ringwraith's form is visible beneath his black cloak.

**MOUTH**
A Ringwraith's Black Breath is poisonous and can give mortals a case of Black Shadow. He speaks in terrible cries that cause terror and despair.

A Ringwraith is one of nine human kings who fell under the spell of Lord Sauron because of their greed. Each Ringwraith has one of the Rings of Power. Sauron's One Ring controls the nine rings, making the Ringwraiths his servants. They become immortal, bound to the power of the One Ring. However, their immortality is unbearable: they live in the shadows and carry darkness with them. Their bodies are visible only to Sauron. Their greatest power is the ability to instill fear. Their poisonous Black Breath gives mortals Black Shadow, which causes nightmares, despair, unconsciousness, and even death.

SIZE

▶ SAURON COMMANDS THE RINGWRAITHS to steal the One Ring from Bilbo the hobbit. Dressed as riders in black, the nine Ringwraiths seek out Bilbo, riding black horses that were bred to endure terror. But Bilbo's nephew Frodo now holds the ring. At the circle of ruins on the hill called Weathertop, the lead Ringwraith stabs Frodo in the arm with a poisoned sword. The wound never completely heals. When the One Ring falls into the fires of Mount Doom, all the Ringwraiths are destroyed.

## Where in the world?

**The Tower of Black Magic, a walled city in J.R.R. Tolkien's realm of Middle-earth, serves as the headquarters for the Ringwraiths.**

MORDOR

## Did you know?

● As servants of Sauron bound to the One Ring, the Ringwraiths are kept in their undead state by their Rings of Power. Destruction of the One Ring is the only way to erase the Ringwraiths.

● When angered, a Ringwraith appears in a fierce fire. Their leader, the witch-king of Angmar, has a sword that can burst into flame.

● Ringwraiths are also referred to as Dark Riders, Black Riders, and the Nine Riders.

● When the Ringwraiths take over the Tower of Black Magic, the once bustling city becomes as silent as a graveyard. No lights appear in any of the windows and a foul smell hangs over the city. Anyone nearing the Tower of Black Magic runs the risk of being driven insane.

# Quasimodo

**EARS**
The tiny ears do not hear well because Quasimodo has grown deaf from the noise of the cathedral's bells.

**FACE**
The hunchback's face does not have a single pleasant feature. A large wart covers Quasimodo's right eye. His uneven teeth, misshapen nose, and bushy eyebrows make a repulsive sight.

**BACK**
His short torso with a large hump between the shoulder blades is balanced by another hump on the chest.

**LEGS**
Quasimodo's crooked legs—ending in clumsy, oversized feet—give him a limping gait.

**HANDS**
Oversized hands give Quasimodo a solid grip on the bell ropes.

Abandoned on the steps of Notre Dame Cathedral, the deformed baby named Quasimodo grows up in the care of archdeacon Frollo. He becomes the bell ringer of Notre Dame. The citizens of Paris regard him as a monster. Pregnant women look away, afraid that their babies will bear his deformities. Quasimodo kidnaps Esmeralda, a gorgeous gypsy girl. She is rescued by Captain Phoebus and falls in love with him. Quasimodo is put on trial and flogged. Esmeralda pities him and brings him water. Now Frollo falls in love with Esmeralda, too. Jealous of Phoebus, Frollo stabs him and flees.

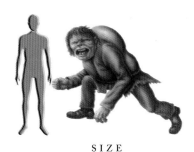

SIZE

▶ PHOEBUS SURVIVES THE STABBING, but Esmeralda is accused of attempting to murder him. She is tried and convicted of the crime. She is on the gallows, seconds away from being hanged, when Quasimodo snatches her from the platform and carries her inside the cathedral. The city leaders vote to remove the gypsy girl from Notre Dame. A group of thieves attack the cathedral to save Esmeralda. Quasimodo thinks they are there to harm her, and flings stones, timber, and molten lead down on top of them.

## Where in the world?

**In Paris, France, during the late 1400s, the bell ringer of Notre Dame Cathedral was none other than the hunchback, Quasimodo.**

PARIS

## Did you know?

● Esmeralda escapes the cathedral but is captured and hanged. Quasimodo blames Frollo for her death and throws the archdeacon off the balcony of Notre Dame.

● Quasimodo is voted the Pope of Fools in the 1482 Festival of Fools for being the ugliest person in Paris.

● The hunchback is named after Quasimodo Sunday, the first Sunday after Easter, which is the day he was abandoned at the cathedral.

● Esmeralda and Quasimodo were switched at birth. A band of gypsies stole Esmeralda from her mother and replaced her with the hideous infant Quasimodo. Quasimodo was abandoned at Notre Dame cathedral and Esmeralda's grieving mother became a recluse. Esmeralda and her mother are reunited just before Esmeralda is executed.

# Phantom of the Opera

**HANDS**
His ice-cold hands smell of death.

**MASK**
A mask conceals the scarred face and damaged nose. Even his own mother was horrified at the sight of him, and he earned his living as a circus freak early in his life.

**BODY**
Erik, the opera phantom, is thin to the point of being bony. His dark coat fits badly and hangs loosely on his lean body.

**SKIN**
Horrible, yellowed skin stretches tightly across his face and hands.

Rumors of a ghost circulate at the Opera Garnier in Paris. The ghost is said to bring havoc and ruin when displeased. An eccentric, deformed musician named Erik lives in secret quarters hidden below the opera house. He sleeps in a coffin and never shows his disfigured face. Erik demands that the managers of the opera pay him a monthly salary and keep a theater box reserved for him at every performance. He threatens disaster if his wishes are not met. When two new managers take over the opera house, they refuse to meet Erik's demands. They think the arrangement is a prank invented by the former managers.

SIZE

▶ ERIK BEGINS TO GIVE VOICE LESSONS TO CHRISTINE, a young soprano. He coaches her through the wall of her dressing room, claiming her dead father sent him as the Angel of Music. Her performances improve and Erik falls in love with her. He puts on a mask to hide his repulsive face and takes her to his lair beneath the opera. As they sing a duet together, Christine cannot contain her curiosity. She rips off Erik's mask to reveal his shocking face.

## Where in the world?

**The hideous phantom terrorizes the Opera Garnier in Paris, France, from his headquarters beneath the elegant building.**

● PARIS

## Did you know?

● When Erik hears of Christine's plan to leave Paris with another man, he kidnaps her from the stage during a performance. He insists that Christine marry him. He warns her that he will blow up the Opera Garnier if she refuses.

● The cavern beneath the opera house where Erik lives was created during its construction. When water was pumped from the foundation pit of the building, a subterranean river was formed.

● Erik maintains a torture chamber beneath the opera house. A stagehand is found hanged near the entrance to the chamber.

● The opera phantom is a murderer and torturer. Erik's weapon of choice is a lasso made of rope. He uses it to strangle or hang his victims.

# Moby Dick

**HEAD**
The whale uses its gigantic, scarred head as a battering ram. His brain is the largest and heaviest known of any mammal, modern or extinct.

**BODY**
Moby Dick is the largest living carnivore on Earth, measuring 60 feet (18 m) long. His weight is estimated at 150 tons (136 tonnes).

**MOUTH**
The jawbone makes up about one-quarter of the whale's overall length. The mouth contains 20 to 26 pairs of cone-shaped teeth measuring 3–8 inches (8–20 cm) long.

Concealed in the depths of the Atlantic Ocean, Moby Dick strikes out unexpectedly. This white whale is the largest toothed animal alive, and no whaling ship can defeat him. Moby Dick fights giant squid, his favorite food, and bears the scars on his skin where the squid's suckers have grabbed him. Captain Ahab and his crew set out in the whaling ship *Pequod* to kill Moby Dick. Ahab wears an ivory peg leg to replace the leg he lost to Moby Dick on a previous hunt. Ahab refers to the vicious whale as a "devil fish."

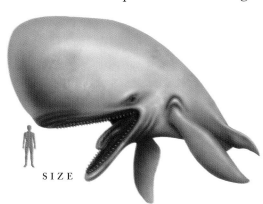

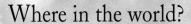

S I Z E

▶ AHAB MUST HAVE REVENGE for his lost leg. For three days, Moby Dick battles the *Pequod*. The whale destroys its hunting boats, rams the ship with his giant head, and sinks it. Only one crew member, named Ishmael, and Captain Ahab remain. Every other member is drowned in the struggle. Ahab hurls harpoons at the beast until he lands one in its hide, but Moby Dick drags Ahab into the cold ocean depths to his death. Ishmael is the sole survivor.

## Where in the world?

**Captain Ahab's ship *Pequod* sails from New Bedford, Massachusetts, into the chilly waters of the Atlantic Ocean to find Moby Dick.**

NEW BEDFORD

## Did you know?

● The *Narrative of the Most Extraordinary and Distressing Shipwreck of the Whale-Ship Essex*, by Owen Chase, inspired Herman Mellville's novel *Moby Dick*. Published in 1821, Chase's account told of the sinking of a ship after it was repeatedly attacked and rammed by a whale.

● In the 1830s, a giant white whale called Mocha Dick was killed off the coast of Chile. Mocha Dick had the very bad habit of attacking whaling ships.

● A whale like Moby Dick can stay underwater for up to two hours without surfacing for air.

● Even though it resembles an enormous fish, the whale is actually a mammal.

# Caliban

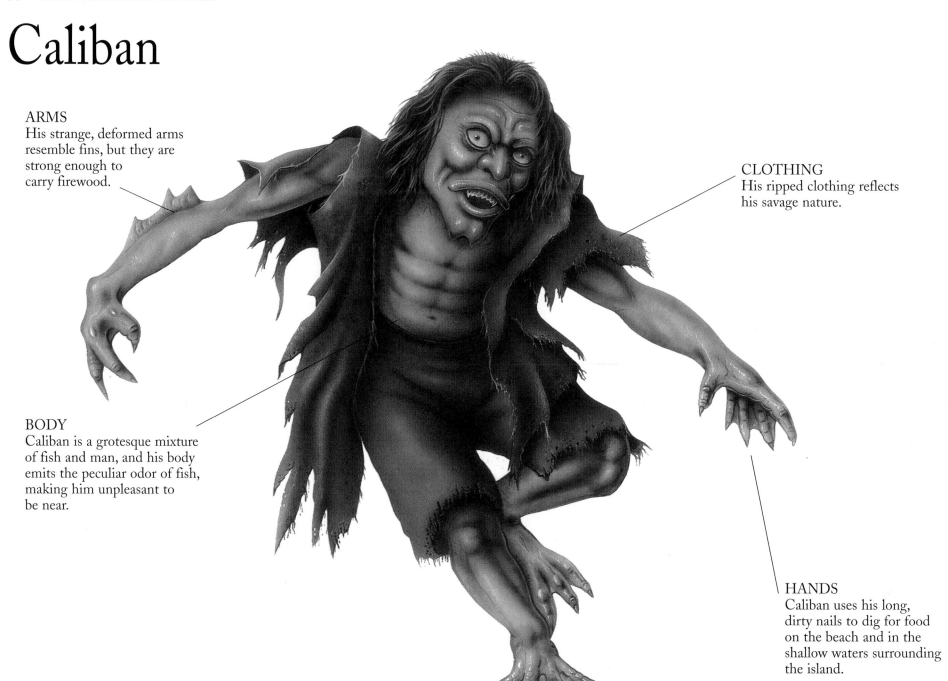

**ARMS**
His strange, deformed arms resemble fins, but they are strong enough to carry firewood.

**CLOTHING**
His ripped clothing reflects his savage nature.

**BODY**
Caliban is a grotesque mixture of fish and man, and his body emits the peculiar odor of fish, making him unpleasant to be near.

**HANDS**
Caliban uses his long, dirty nails to dig for food on the beach and in the shallow waters surrounding the island.

When Prospero and his daughter Miranda are stranded on an island, they discover Caliban, the son of a witch and a demon. Caliban is referred to as a mooncalf because of the moon's sinister effects on his development. He looks like a cross between a fish and a man. Prospero and Miranda teach Caliban to speak English. In return, Caliban teaches them how to survive on the island. Caliban cannot rise above his beastly nature, and he attacks Miranda. As punishment for behaving like a brute, Prospero makes Caliban his slave and treats him harshly. Resentful, Caliban tries to raise a rebellion against his master Prospero.

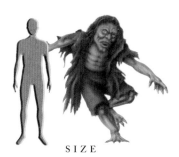

SIZE

► CALIBAN WAS THE ONLY INHABITANT OF HIS ISLAND before the shipwreck landed others there. He feels that Prospero has cheated him of his island, and begins plotting to murder him. Caliban's plot involves bashing in Prospero's head as he sleeps and burning all his books. He encourages Stefano, a member of the crew of the shipwrecked vessel, to kill Prospero and take over the island, but the plan fails. Caliban once again swears allegiance to Prospero.

## Where in the world?

**Prospero and Miranda are stranded on Caliban's magical island in the Mediterranean Sea, somewhere between Tunisia and Italy.**

● CALIBAN'S ISLAND

## Did you know?

● Prospero was in line to be the Duke of Milan, but his jealous brother set him and Miranda adrift in a boat to get rid of them. They are able to survive because a friend made sure that there were plenty of food, books, and supplies on board. The boat is also secretly reinforced to make it seaworthy. Prospero and Miranda drift until they come ashore on Caliban's island.

● These characters first appeared in William Shakespeare's play *The Tempest*. It was first performed in 1611 for England's King James I.

● *Forbidden Planet*, a 1956 science fiction movie, is an adaptation of *The Tempest* set in the future on the planet Altair IV.

# Macbeth's Witches

**HANDS**
Storms and spirits are raised with spells cast by their clawed hands. They stir their cauldron and summon apparitions with predictions that awaken a thirst for power in Macbeth and give him false hope.

**FACES**
Withered and wild-looking, the three witches all have skinny faces with large, bent noses and warts.

**MOUTHS**
Thin lips stretch across rotting teeth that give off a foul odor. The witches' terrible, cackling laughter echoes across the moors and turns peaceful dreams into nightmares.

**CLOTHING**
Their dark, ragged clothing and pointed hats identify the wicked hags as witches.

Macbeth, who is the Thane (Baron) of Glamis, and his general Banquo encounter three witches. They tell Banquo that he will father a line of kings. To his surprise, they call Macbeth "Thane of Cawdor" and tell him he shall be a king. Soon thereafter, Macbeth becomes Thane of Cawdor. Their prediction has come true, and he now begins to think of being king. He kills King Duncan to secure the throne and hires assassins to kill Banquo and his family, but Banquo's son escapes. Banquo's ghost haunts Macbeth, and Macbeth's wife, Lady Macbeth, goes insane from the guilt.

SIZE

▶ MACBETH APPROACHES THE WITCHES AGAIN. The weird sisters gather around a cauldron, where they conjure three spirits with three warnings. The first apparition is a head equipped with weapons that warns him to beware of Macduff. The second spirit is a bloody child, who says that no one born of a woman shall harm Macbeth. The witches' third awful vision is of a child wearing a crown and holding a branch in his hand. The crowned child says that Macbeth shall never be defeated until Birnam Wood comes to Dunsinane Hill.

## Where in the world?

● SCOTLAND

**The weird sisters stir their bubbling cauldron in the darkness on Scotland's desolate moors.**

## Did you know?

● Soldiers under Macduff's command cut large branches from trees in Birnam Wood. They use these as a disguise to conceal the size of their army as they march against Macbeth in the castle on Dunsinane Hill.

● Macbeth is killed by Macduff despite the spirit's prediction that Macbeth cannot be harmed by anyone born of a woman. This is possible because Macduff was born by cesarean section rather than by natural childbirth.

● True to the apparition's prediction, Banquo's descendents go on to become rulers of England.

● The evil broth in the witches' cauldron contains eye of newt, toe of frog, wool of bat, and tongue of dog. Pieces of snake, toad, lizard, and owl are added to the mixture as well.

# Rumpelstiltskin

**HEAD**
His pointed hat and pointed ears identify Rumpelstiltskin as a dwarf.

**HANDS**
Rumpelstiltskin's swift hands have the magical ability to spin straw into gold. They can also whip up nightmares to haunt a human's sleep.

**ARMS**
The dwarf's wiry arms possess superhuman strength, enabling him to tear his own body in half.

**FEET**
He is a skilled dancer, so his traditional pointed dwarf shoes do not interfere with his dance around his campfire in the woods at night.

A poor miller hoping to impress the king boasts that his daughter can spin straw into gold. The king shuts her in a tower room with nothing but straw and a spinning wheel. She is expected to spin the straw into gold by morning. If she fails, she will be killed. But the young woman cannot spin straw into gold. She begins to despair, and then a dwarf named Rumpelstiltskin appears in the locked room. In exchange for her necklace, the dwarf uses his magical powers to spin the straw into gold. Impressed, the king tells her to do it again and locks her in the tower room with even more straw on the second night.

SIZE

► RUMPELSTILTSKIN APPEARS AGAIN, and this time she trades him her ring for spinning the straw into gold for her. The king demands that she repeat the trick a third night and locks her up one last time. Now she has nothing left to trade the dwarf, so she promises her first-born child to him if he will spin the straw into gold. The king marries her. Nothing more is heard of Rumpelstiltskin until she bears her first child and the dwarf comes to claim the baby.

## Where in the world?

***Rumpelstiltskin* is one of the numerous fairy tales collected by the Brothers Grimm in Germany during the early 1800s.**

GERMANY

## Did you know?

• The young woman offers Rumpelstiltskin all her riches if he will allow her to keep her baby. He agrees that she may keep her child if she can guess his name. He gives her three days for the task. A messenger overhears Rumpelstiltskin singing a rhyme about his name and reports the dwarf's name to the woman.

• When she correctly guesses his name, Rumpelstiltskin is enraged. He stomps his right foot so hard that it is buried into the ground up to his waist. In his fury, he grabs his own left foot in both hands and rips himself in two.

• Rumpelstiltskin appears in the animated movie *Shrek the Third*, as a member of Prince Charming's army of villains.

# Witch

**BODY**
The witch is a bent old hag with a crooked back that requires her to walk with a cane. She cannot move quickly and relies on trickery or spells to capture children.

**HANDS**
She uses her bony hands and clawlike nails to pick the last bits of meat from the bones of children she has eaten.

**EYES**
Her eyes cannot see well, enabling Hansel to trick her when she checks how fat he is getting.

**NOSE**
A keen sense of smell enables the awful witch to sniff the air and smell Hansel and Gretel approaching from a great distance.

Deep in a forest in southern Germany lives a cannibal witch, who dines on the tender flesh of lost children. Hansel and Gretel, the children of a poor woodcutter, are abandoned deep in the forest when there is not enough food for their family to survive. Hansel cleverly leaves a trail of breadcrumbs when he and his sister are led into the forest, thinking they can follow it back home. However, the birds eat the breadcrumb trail and the children are lost. They find a gingerbread house with sugar windows and a cake roof. The hungry children start to nibble at the house, not knowing it is the home of an evil witch.

SIZE

▶ THE WITCH INVITES HANSEL AND GRETEL IN FOR A MEAL. She imprisons Hansel in a shed and forces Gretel to cook for her brother so that he will fatten up. Hansel eats rich food every day, but Gretel is fed only scraps. The day arrives when the witch is ready to eat Hansel. She fires up her oven and orders Gretel to get in it to test how hot it is. Sensing a trick, Gretel shoves the witch in and slams the door shut on her.

## Where in the world?

GERMANY

**Hansel and Gretel live on the outskirts of the magical Black Forest in southwestern Germany.**

## Did you know?

● Every day, the nearsighted witch tested how fat Hansel was getting by feeling his finger. Hansel fooled her into thinking he was staying thin by holding out a small chicken bone instead of his finger for her to feel.

● Because of Gretel's quick thinking, the witch is baked in her own oven. Gretel frees Hansel from the shed and they stuff their pockets with jewels from the witch's house. They return to their father's house with the riches, and no one in their family ever goes hungry again.

● An operatic version of the story titled *Hänsel und Gretel* was written by German composer Engelbert Humperdinck (1854–1921) in 1891.

# Evil Queen

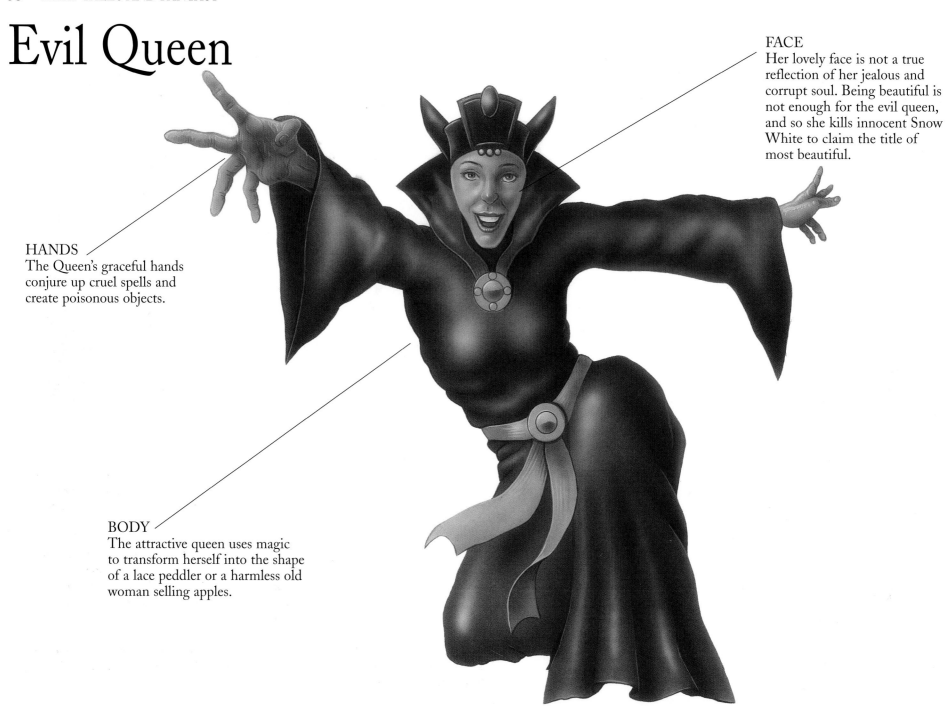

**FACE**
Her lovely face is not a true reflection of her jealous and corrupt soul. Being beautiful is not enough for the evil queen, and so she kills innocent Snow White to claim the title of most beautiful.

**HANDS**
The Queen's graceful hands conjure up cruel spells and create poisonous objects.

**BODY**
The attractive queen uses magic to transform herself into the shape of a lace peddler or a harmless old woman selling apples.

A proud, beautiful queen with supernatural powers asks her magic mirror the same question each day: "Who is the fairest in the land?" The mirror always replies that the queen is the fairest in the land. One day, though, the mirror responds differently, saying the fairest in the land is Snow White. The jealous queen sends Snow White into the forest with a huntsman. He has orders to kill Snow White and bring back her lungs and liver as proof that she is dead. The huntsman pities Snow White and lets her live. He kills a wild boar and takes its lungs and liver to the queen. The evil queen eats the lungs and liver, believing they are Snow White's.

S I Z E

▶ SEVEN FRIENDLY DWARVES TAKE SNOW WHITE INTO THEIR HOME. The next time the evil queen asks her mirror the daily question, it replies "Snow White," and the queen knows that the girl is still alive. The queen disguises herself as a peddler selling lace. She wraps Snow White so tightly in laces that the girl cannot breathe and faints. The dwarves save Snow White by cutting the laces away. The queen knows that Snow White lives because the mirror still identifies her as the fairest.

## Where in the world?

GERMANY

**The evil queen holds her grudge against the beautiful Snow White from her castle high up on a hill in Germany.**

## Did you know?

• The evil queen produces a poisoned comb, but the dwarves pull the comb from Snow White's hair and save her. Once again, the mirror's answer that Snow White is the fairest confirms she is alive.

• Using black magic, the vain queen poisons an apple that kills Snow White. The dwarves place Snow White in a glass coffin on a hilltop, where she lies for years but does not decay. A passing prince asks if he may have the beautiful girl in the coffin. When his servants move the coffin, they jostle it and the bite of poisoned apple is jarred loose from Snow White's mouth. Snow White comes back to life.

• The evil queen attends the wedding of Snow White and the prince. A pair of iron slippers is heated in a fire and the evil queen is forced to dance in the red-hot shoes until she drops to the floor, dead.

# Mordred

**HELMET**
Made of forged steel, the helmet protects Mordred's head and neck from sword cuts and arrow strikes.

**HEART**
Mordred is completely lacking in loyalty. His cold heart is filled with malice toward Arthur and his knights.

**SHIELD**
His shield blocks blows from his enemies' swords. Its layers of wood covered with leather protect Mordred during battle.

**SWORD**
He slashes and cuts his way through battle, using the sharp, pointed tip of his sword for thrusting. Mordred uses this sword to fatally wound King Arthur.

**ARMOR**
Mordred's plate armor is practically sword-proof. The only way he can be killed is by a well-aimed sword thrust to a joint where there is only weaker chain mail to protect him.

Sir Mordred the Traitor is a warrior chief. His betrayals lead first to the downfall of King Arthur, and then to the destruction of the Round Table. Mordred is unkind to the younger knights, mocking them publicly. King Arthur is unaware that Queen Guinevere and Sir Lancelot are in love with each other. Mordred exposes them to Arthur and, according to the law, Arthur must now put to death his queen and dearest friend. Lancelot flees, though he returns to rescue Guinevere from being burnt at the stake. Arthur travels to France to fight Lancelot, and makes Mordred his deputy ruler.

SIZE

▶ WHILE ARTHUR IS AWAY, Mordred falsely announces that Arthur is dead. Mordred then seizes the crown and forms an alliance with the Saxons, giving them a hold in Britain in return for their aid and support. Mordred tries to take Guinevere as his wife. She pretends to agree to the arrangement, but hides from Mordred in the Tower of London. Guinevere and a loyal garrison withstand a siege by Mordred's troops. Arthur returns to England and battles Mordred. Arthur kills Mordred, but Arthur himself is mortally wounded during combat.

## Where in the world?

**According to Arthurian legend, Sir Mordred betrayed his king and destroyed the fellowship of the Knights of the Round Table in Camelot, allegedly located in Cornwall, England.**

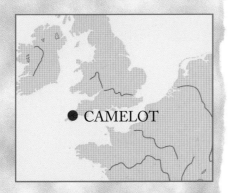

● CAMELOT

## Did you know?

● The wizard Merlin predicted that a child born on May Day would kill King Arthur and wipe out his kingdom. To protect himself, Arthur had all children born on May Day gathered up and sent out to sea on a leaky ship. All of the children drowned but one. The lone survivor was Mordred.

● Mordred is officially King Arthur's nephew, but there are rumors that he is actually a son that Arthur refuses to claim as his own.

● Mordred violates every requirement in the knights' code of chivalry, including committing treason, murdering, and engaging in battle over wrongful quarrels.

# Medusa

## FACE
She once stunned men with her striking looks. After the goddess Athena punishes Medusa and turns her into a shocking monster, her cold, frightful gaze stuns them to death.

## HAIR
Her long, lustrous hair changes into a slithering mass of poisonous snakes. Any person who manages to approach Medusa without looking at her is still in danger from the aggressive snakes that strike at anything that moves.

## MOUTH
Medusa's breath has a foul odor similar to the scent of decaying flesh. Her white teeth narrow to points, like a snake's fangs. If anyone manages to get near her without dying, her teeth are capable of flaying the flesh from human bones.

## BODY
Medusa has the same body as when she was a beauty. However, with one well-aimed blow of Perseus' mighty sword, her body and terrible head part ways forever.

Once a beautiful woman in Greek mythology, Medusa is transformed by a jealous goddess into one of the most dangerous creatures in history. The god Poseidon falls in love with the gorgeous Medusa and meets with her in the temple of the goddess Athena. The goddess is furious that her sacred temple is used for anything other than worship. As punishment, Medusa's flowing hair is turned into a nest of writhing, spitting snakes, and her lovely face becomes hideous. The formerly attractive and charming Medusa is now a frightening outcast, feared by everyone. Anyone who gazes at Medusa directly is immediately turned to stone. Her looks literally kill.

SIZE

▶ PERSEUS, WHO WAS RAISED BY PRIESTS FROM ATHENA'S TEMPLE, promises to bring King Polydectes and Athena the head of Medusa. Perseus quietly creeps up to Medusa as she is sleeping. He uses his polished shield as a mirror because looking directly at her means instant death. With her terrible image reflected in his shield, he swings his sturdy sword and cuts off her head with one powerful blow. Even in death, her severed head has the power to turn anyone who looks upon it to stone.

## Where in the world?

**In ancient Libya, on Africa's northern coast, citizens had to be careful not to make eye contact with this ugly, snake-haired lady.**

LIBYA

## Did you know?

● Perseus places Medusa's head in a pouch and takes it out during battles to turn his enemies to stone.

● Medusa's head is later placed on Athena's shield as a symbol of the goddess' power.

● When Perseus cuts off Medusa's head, the blood that is spilled creates the multitude of snakes that inhabit Africa to this day.

● Medusa's blood changes into red coral when it falls onto the ocean floor.

● When King Atlas of Mauritania threatens Perseus and refuses to allow him into his palace, Perseus shows Atlas the severed head of Medusa. At the sight of Medusa's head, King Atlas is changed into a mountain in the desert of Africa. Mount Atlas stands there today, frozen eternally in place.

# Hydra

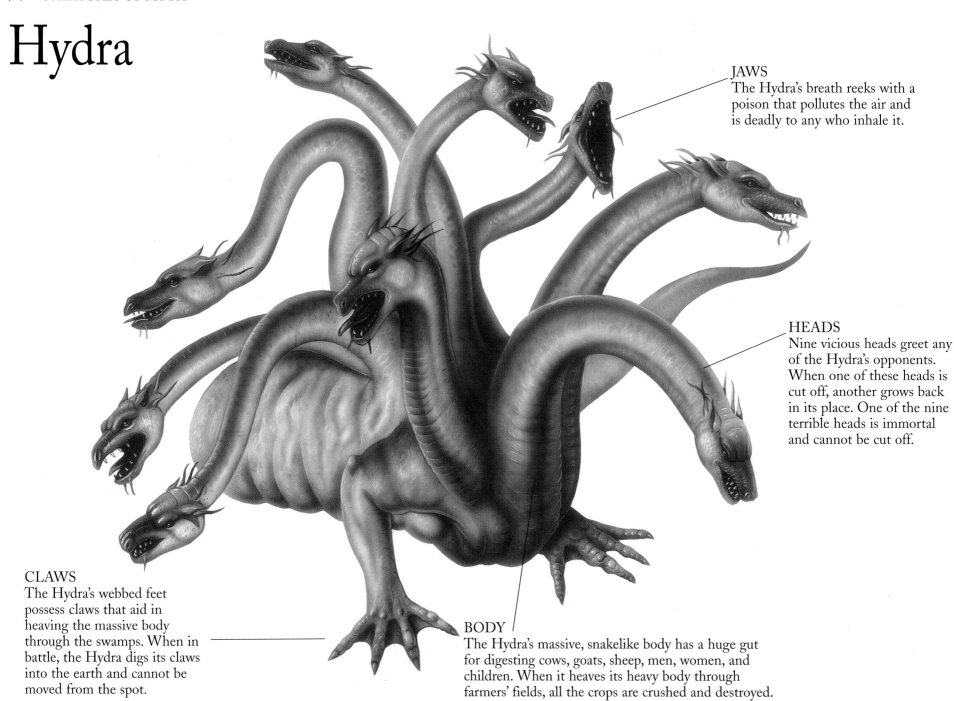

**JAWS**
The Hydra's breath reeks with a poison that pollutes the air and is deadly to any who inhale it.

**HEADS**
Nine vicious heads greet any of the Hydra's opponents. When one of these heads is cut off, another grows back in its place. One of the nine terrible heads is immortal and cannot be cut off.

**CLAWS**
The Hydra's webbed feet possess claws that aid in heaving the massive body through the swamps. When in battle, the Hydra digs its claws into the earth and cannot be moved from the spot.

**BODY**
The Hydra's massive, snakelike body has a huge gut for digesting cows, goats, sheep, men, women, and children. When it heaves its heavy body through farmers' fields, all the crops are crushed and destroyed.

Ancient Lerna conceals an entrance to the underworld, which is guarded by the terrible, nine-headed Hydra. Its poisonous breath fouls the air with a stench strong enough to kill a man. The Hydra also ranges through the countryside, flattening crops and terrifying locals. Neither livestock nor citizens are safe from the beast with nine ravenous heads. If any one of its heads is cut off, another immediately grows back in its place. Many people die of fright just from the sight of the Hydra. Everyone in Lerna believes that the Hydra cannot be destroyed until the arrival of Hercules, who is determined to kill the menace.

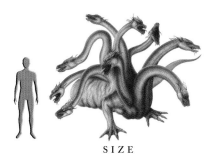

SIZE

▶ HERCULES FIRES FLAMING ARROWS INTO THE HYDRA'S LAIR to draw it out into the open. He begins chopping off Hydra heads with his sword, only to discover that they grow back as fast as he can lop them off. With a flaming torch in hand, Hercules's nephew comes to his aid by scorching the wound as soon as Hercules cuts off a head. When the bleeding stumps are burned, the heads cannot grow back. However, one of the Hydra's heads is immortal and cannot be removed by any weapon that a person can make.

## Where in the world?

**The Hydra could be found in the swamps and lake near the ancient city of Lerna in Argolis, Greece.**

LERNA

## Did you know?

● To kill the Hydra's one immortal head, Hercules crushes its skull with an enormous club, and then rips off the head with his bare hands. He buries the head beneath a large rock, where it can no longer trouble anyone.

● Hercules dips his arrowheads in the Hydra's poisonous blood, making them lethal.

● When Hercules approaches the Hydra, he covers his mouth and nose with a cloth to avoid inhaling its lethal fumes.

● Killing the Hydra was the second labor of Hercules, a series of 12 tasks assigned to him by the king who sat on the throne that was originally intended for Hercules.

● The Hydra's siblings are the Chimaera and Cerberus.

# Cerberus

**TAIL**
Even Cerberus' tail is poisonous, making it as dangerous as the three howling heads. A single lash from his snakelike tail is fatal.

**HEADS**
Cerberus' blood-red eyes, acute hearing, and slobbering mouths lined with 126 razor-sharp teeth are three times as dangerous as any dog's on Earth.

**BODY**
The muscular body is designed for sprinting and springing on prey. Cerberus can run for an unusually long time without tiring, making it impossible to escape from him on foot.

**MOUTHS**
Cerberus' spittle burns and poisons the earth. His brassy voice emits a bloodcurdling howl. The trio of merciless heads is intent on mutilating prey.

Cerberus, the three-headed hound with a snake's tail, guards the entrance to the underworld to prevent the living from entering and the dead from escaping. If the dead attempt to escape, they are devoured. Living visitors who attempt to enter the underworld risk the same fate. His watchful eyes, keen hearing, and foul temper make it impossible to sneak past him. Those who do get by him accomplish the task through trickery. Orpheus, one of the best-known musicians in Greek mythology, can charm wild beasts with his songs. Playing a song on his lyre, Orpheus lulls Cerberus to sleep and creeps past to seek his beloved wife.

SIZE

▶ THE HERO HERCULES IS GIVEN THE TASK OF CAPTURING CERBERUS as the last of the 12 labors assigned to him by the king. The rulers of the underworld give Hercules permission to capture Cerberus on the condition that he does not harm the dog. Hercules wrestles the evil creature into submission using brute strength alone. He seizes the dog by two of its throats and hauls the struggling animal out of the underworld. When Hercules brings Cerberus out of Hades, the king is so frightened that he hides in a large storage jar.

## Where in the world?

**Cerberus stands guard at the entrance to Hades, the underworld of Greek mythology, which is populated by the dead.**

● GREECE

## Did you know?

● Once Hercules proved to the king that he could capture Cerberus, he returned the terrible dog to his post in Hades.

● The name *Cerberus* means "demon of the pit."

● Hades, the land of the dead in Greek mythology, lies beneath the ground. The River Styx is the boundary between the underworld and the earth. Styx represents hate and is said to wrap around Hades nine times. Cerberus, feared by the gods themselves, can be found guarding the gates of Hades.

● Poisonous plants sprout from the foam that drips from his trio of snarling mouths.

# Chimaera

**BODY**
Part lion, part goat, the Chimaera has an impenetrable hide that cannot be pierced by sword or spear.

**HEADS**
With three mouths to feed, the Chimaera is always hungry. The serpent head, the lion head, and the goat head sometimes torch their prey before eating it. More often than not, they consume their terrified victims alive.

**REAR LEGS**
The rear legs of a goat give the Chimaera uncanny agility. It scrambles easily over all types of terrain in search of a target for its rage.

**JAWS**
The Chimaera's mighty jaws spew forth a ferocious stream of fire that converts forests into kindling, homes into smoking ruins, and crops into useless ash.

**FRONT LEGS**
The powerful forelegs of a lion are necessary to support the Chimaera's three hulking heads. Its claws are handy for ripping flesh it has not already gulped down or roasted.

The ghastly Chimaera, once the pet of the king of Caria, escapes. Rampaging within the king's court, it terrorizes everyone it meets with its three fearsome heads: the head of a goat, the head of a lion, and the head of a serpent. Continually vomiting flames, it ravages the countryside and sets fire to everything in sight. When the Chimaera reaches Lycia, it sears the land with its fiery breath and consumes every living thing that crosses its path. Not only is the beast swift-footed and strong, it is immortal as well. No weapon made by humans can harm it.

SIZE

▶ BELLEROPHON, ONE OF THE GREATEST HEROES OF GREEK MYTHOLOGY, is sent by the king of Lycia to slay the Chimaera. Riding his winged horse Pegasus, courageous Bellerophon flies high above the Chimaera's searing flames. The monster's breath is hot enough to melt the hero's spear, so Bellerophon places a block of lead on the tip of his spear. He flies straight at the beast and thrusts the lead-tipped spear into the Chimaera's throat. Its flaming breath melts the lead, which seals the Chimaera's throat shut. The Chimaera quickly suffocates.

## Where in the world?

**Residents of ancient Lycia, which lies on the southwestern coast of modern-day Turkey, lived in fear of the fire-breathing Chimaera.**

LYCIA

## Did you know?

● The Chimaera claims both the Hydra and Cerberus as its siblings. Their parents specialized in producing monstrous beasts with multiple heads.

● Athena, the warrior goddess, gave Bellerophon a golden bridle in a dream as he slept in her temple. Waking to find the bridle still in his hands, he used it to capture Pegasus, the winged horse he would ride to face the Chimaera.

● The Chimaera left the bones of his many victims strewn across a local mountainside. Lycia was once a happy place but now the inhabitants lived with the constant fear that they or a loved one would be snatched up and consumed by the Chimaera.

● In some accounts, the Chimaera has the head of a lion, the body of a goat, and the tail of a snake.

# Harpy

**WINGS**
Wings as powerful as an eagle's enable the Harpy to fly considerable distances while bearing the weight of a heavy human in her talons.

**FACE**
Her spiteful nature shows in the Harpy's hideous face. Piercing shrieks issuing from her mouth can cause temporary deafness in anyone nearby.

**TAIL**
Her massive tail acts as a rudder during flight, balancing and steering the Harpy as she swoops down on her victims. When the tail dips downward, she stops short to grab her prey.

**CLAWS**
The oversized talons are designed for perching and snatching food from the hungry. They are also useful for transporting the uncooperative to the underworld.

**BODY**
A Harpy's vulture body emits a terrible stench that clings to everything she touches.

Three winged death spirits called Harpies loom large in Greek mythology. With the faces of women and bodies of vultures, they shriek, peck, and nag. Relentless tormentors, they spoil everything they touch with their filth. Circling the skies, singing their songs of discontent, they harass sailors on passing ships. The god of the underworld sends them on terrible errands, dispatching them to seize anyone unwilling to die. The Harpy flies around her prey, screeching and diving at him. Once her victim is terrified senseless, she sinks her claws into him and delivers him to the gates of Hades.

SIZE

▶ A GREEK NAMED PHINEAS, who has the gift of prophecy, angers the god Zeus. Zeus feels that Phineas reveals too many details of the gods' plans. Zeus punishes Phineas by blinding him and leaving him on an island. A lavish buffet of food is set for Phineas on the island, but the Harpies make sure he never eats a scrap of it. The noisy Harpies constantly pester Phineas, stealing food from his hands and ruining the leftovers so he is unable to eat.

## Where in the world?

**Off the western shore of Greece in the Mediterranean Sea, the Harpies roost in the rocky Strofades Islands.**

● STROFADES

## Did you know?

● Eventually, two winged heroes known as the Boreads drive the Harpies away. The rainbow goddess Iris asks that the Harpies not be harmed. In return for their safety, Iris promises that the Harpies shall never again bother Phineas.

● The name *Harpy* is derived from the Greek word for "snatcher."

● The Strofades Islands, the traditional home of the Harpies, are a destination for avid birdwatchers hoping to catch a glimpse of rare waterfowl.

● Ill-tempered, greedy people are referred to as "harpies."

● In Dante's fourteenth-century poem "Inferno," Harpies eternally taunt people who have died greedy.

# Siren

**HEAD**
Though she is a miserable, treacherous beast, the Siren has the head of a beautiful woman.

**MOUTH**
The Siren is the most accomplished singer in Greek mythology. Melodies that no mortal man can resist issue from her lips.

**WINGS**
Bird's wings carry the Siren between islands and enable her to fly above the heads of defenseless sailors, singing her fatal tune.

**CLAWS**
Using her bird claws, the Siren and her feathered sisters scavenge the carcasses that litter their islands. Clawed feet are necessary for perching on craggy rocks and ships' rigging.

Sailors passing by the three rocky islands off the coast of Italy sometimes hear tunes so haunting and sweet that they forget their homes, grow helpless, and crash their ships on the rocks. The musicians are the Sirens, three bird-women who lure sailors to their deaths with their songs. Their islands appear white from the heaps of sun-bleached bones of sailors long ago lured to their doom. Orpheus,

S I Z E

the father of songs and inventor of the lyre in Greek mythology, survives the Siren song. Sailing past their islands, he plays his lyre so loudly that he drowns out their melody. One sailor hears their song and plunges overboard, but he is saved before he can be tempted toward his own death.

▶ ODYSSEUS, THE KING OF ITHACA, grows curious about the Siren's song. He orders the crew aboard his ship to stuff their ears with beeswax so that they cannot be mesmerized to death. Odysseus himself is strapped to the mast of his ship, ensuring that he can hear the Sirens singing but will not be able to throw himself overboard. When he hears their bewitching song, he orders his crew to untie him, but they cannot hear his order. The ship sails on out of range of their song and all aboard are safe.

## Where in the world?

According to Greek myth, the Sirens make their home on three rocky islands called Li Galli. Ancient sailors passing east of the island of Capri, off the southwestern coast of Italy, had to beware.

● CAPRI

## Did you know?

● Prophecy states that the Sirens are fated to die when a sailor who hears their song passes unharmed. When Odysseus survives hearing them sing, the Sirens fling themselves into the sea and drown.

● The Sirens sing their beautiful song while swooping through the air or while standing on their islands among the rotting corpses of men they lured to destruction.

● In classical art, Sirens are sometimes depicted as women with the wings and legs of birds. In some paintings, they are shown as mermaids playing the lyre or flute.

● Li Galli, the islands of the Sirens, were once known as Le Sirenuse in honor of the Sirens.

# Sphinx

**WINGS**
Large eagle's wings enable the Sphinx to swoop down upon anyone answering her riddle incorrectly. After devouring a human, she flies back to her perch and awaits her next victim.

**BODY**
Her robust lion's body gives the Sphinx speed, stealth, and unbelievable strength for pinning her victims.

**HEAD**
An Egyptian headdress and false beard are a remnant of the Sphinx's origins in Egypt, where sphinxes were guardians representing the power of the pharaoh.

**PAWS**
The Sphinx stands on her victim's neck with her mighty lion's paws and chokes the life from him. Sharp claws rake the flesh easily from the human body.

A demon of death, destruction, and bad luck, the Sphinx sits high atop a rock and poses a riddle to all young men who pass by. Those who cannot answer correctly are killed. This winged lion with a woman's head swoops down and pounces upon her victim. After strangling him to death, she eats him. Her riddle is: "Which creature has one voice but goes on four feet in the morning, two feet at noon, and three feet in the evening?" When the Sphinx slaughters King Creon's son, Creon offers his kingdom and the hand of his sister Jocasta in marriage to anyone who can answer the Sphinx's riddle.

SIZE

▶ OEDIPUS ARRIVES ON THE SCENE and faces the Sphinx. She recites her riddle to Oedipus and readies herself to pounce upon him, but he answers, "A man. In childhood, he crawls on his hands and knees; in adulthood, he walks upright; in old age, he uses a cane." Furious that he has answered her riddle correctly, the Sphinx flings herself from her high perch and dies when she lands on the jagged rocks below. Oedipus is awarded Jocasta as his bride, and it is here that his troubles begin.

## Where in the world?

**The Sphinx originally comes from the ancient kingdom of Egypt, dating from the third millenium B.C. The Greek hero Oedipus encountered the Sphinx while on his travels.**

EGYPT ●

## Did you know?

● An oracle predicts Oedipus will kill his father and marry his mother. His father fears the prophecy and abandons Oedipus. Oedipus grows up not knowing he is adopted. On the road one day, Oedipus kills a man during an argument, unaware that the man is his father. Later he marries Jocasta, not knowing she is his mother.

● A plague falls upon the people of Thebes as punishment for having a king and queen who are son and mother. When Oedipus finds out the terrible truth about his parents, he blinds himself. It seems the cursed Sphinx has had her revenge after all.

● Other varieties of sphinxes resemble ram-headed lions or hawk-headed lions.

● The Sphinx's name is derived from a Greek word that means "to strangle."

# Grendel

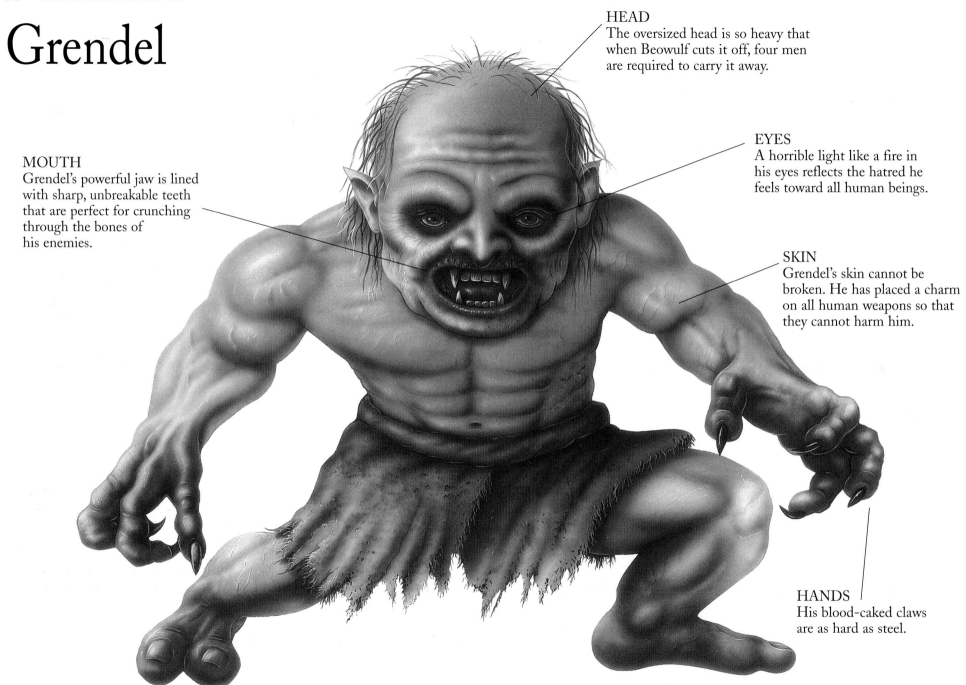

**HEAD**
The oversized head is so heavy that when Beowulf cuts it off, four men are required to carry it away.

**EYES**
A horrible light like a fire in his eyes reflects the hatred he feels toward all human beings.

**MOUTH**
Grendel's powerful jaw is lined with sharp, unbreakable teeth that are perfect for crunching through the bones of his enemies.

**SKIN**
Grendel's skin cannot be broken. He has placed a charm on all human weapons so that they cannot harm him.

**HANDS**
His blood-caked claws are as hard as steel.

As an outcast, Grendel walks in desolate places on the fringes of society. Angered by the sounds of singing and celebration coming from the feasting hall, Grendel wages war for 12 years against the Danes. A furious and hungry creature, he leaves behind scenes of carnage and bloody footprints. Killing more than 30 warriors in the feasting hall, he drags away their bodies to eat them in his swamp lair. Grendel cannot be stopped. He has placed a magical charm on all human weapons, which means that no knife, arrow, spear, or sword can harm him. The king and his people abandon the feasting hall. Only the hero Beowulf is unafraid.

SIZE

▶ BEOWULF AND HIS MEN spend the night in the feasting hall. As they sleep, Grendel enters and attacks, devouring one of Beowulf's soldiers. Beowulf is only pretending to sleep. He leaps up and grasps Grendel's hand in a death grip. Beowulf's men come to his aid, but their weapons cannot pierce Grendel's skin. Beowulf summons all his strength and, using only his bare hands, rips Grendel's arm off. Grendel retreats to his swamp to die, leaving a trail of blood behind him.

## Where in the world?

The outcast Grendel and his man-eating habits are known throughout Geatland, a region in the south of Sweden.

GEATLAND

## Did you know?

● Grendel dies in his cave beneath the swamp. Grendel's mother, who is also a terrible beast, attacks the feasting hall, seeking revenge for the death of her son. Beowulf tracks her to the swamp cave, where she battles Beowulf and comes close to defeating the great hero. Fortunately, Beowulf notices a sword and uses it to kill Grendel's mother.

● Beowulf finds Grendel's corpse in the cave, removes the head with the sword, and keeps it as a battle trophy, proving his victory over the dreadful menace. The king rewards Beowulf for ridding Geatland of Grendel and his gruesome mother.

● Grendel is a descendent of Cain, the first murderer in the Bible.

# Fenrir

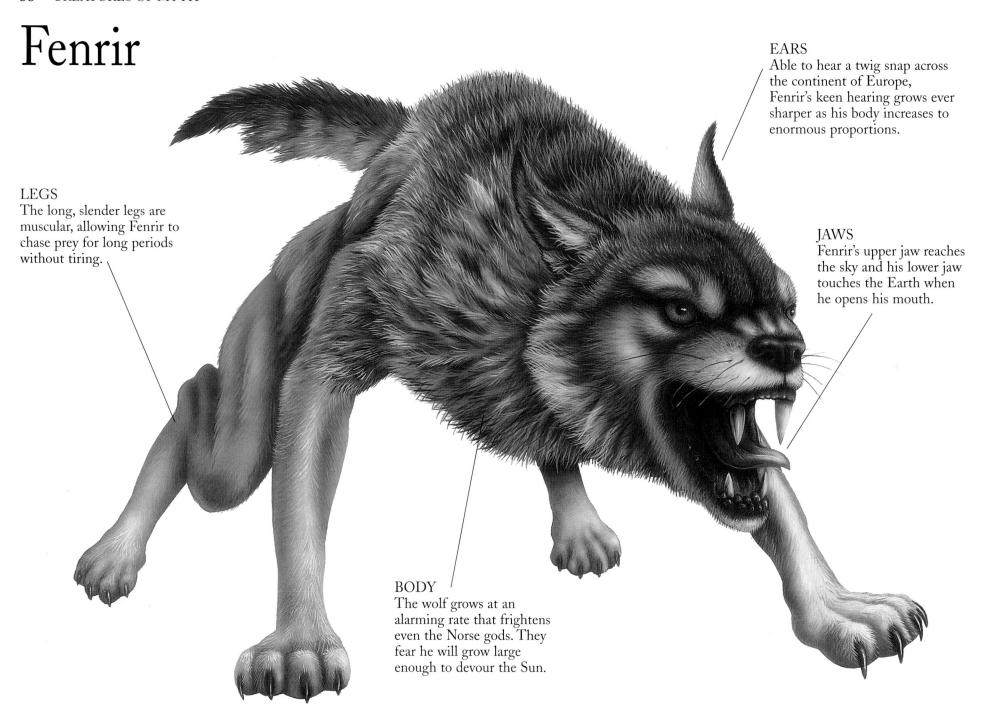

**EARS**
Able to hear a twig snap across the continent of Europe, Fenrir's keen hearing grows ever sharper as his body increases to enormous proportions.

**LEGS**
The long, slender legs are muscular, allowing Fenrir to chase prey for long periods without tiring.

**JAWS**
Fenrir's upper jaw reaches the sky and his lower jaw touches the Earth when he opens his mouth.

**BODY**
The wolf grows at an alarming rate that frightens even the Norse gods. They fear he will grow large enough to devour the Sun.

A prophecy states that the gigantic wolf Fenrir and his family will one day destroy the world. Even the gods fear Fenrir, the child of a giantess and Loki, the Father of All Lies. Odin, the chief god in Norse mythology, hopes to tame Fenrir, but all the other gods shrink at the sight of the wolf. Only Tyr, the god of war, is brave enough to feed the rapidly growing beast. Fenrir's size and fierceness increase daily. The gods bind the hungry wolf with chains, but twice he breaks loose. Elves create a magic ribbon that will hold Fenrir. The powerful wolf does not trust the gods and senses the ribbon may contain magic beyond his powers.

SIZE

▶ FENRIR INSISTS THAT ONE OF THE GODS PLACE A HAND IN HIS MOUTH as a gesture of good faith that no magic will be used against him. Tyr is the only one brave enough to place his hand in the wolf's mouth. When Fenrir realizes he cannot break the magic ribbon, he bites off Tyr's hand. Fenrir fights against his restraints, but the gods prop open his mouth with a sword to keep him from biting. The blood and drool that run from his jaws form a rushing river.

## Where in the world?

SCANDINAVIA

**Fenrir's terrible howls can be heard throughout the Scandinavian countries of Norway, Sweden, and Denmark.**

## Did you know?

● Fenrir bursts free to take his revenge during the battle at the end of the world. He belches fire and smoke, creating clouds of deadly vapors that fill heaven and Earth with his poisonous breath.

● Fenrir defeats Odin by growing larger and larger as they fight. Once Fenrir's jaws embrace all the space between heaven and Earth, he swallows Odin whole.

● Odin's son Vidar steps on Fenrir's lower jaw, seizes the wolf's upper jaw in his hands, and rips the dreadful monster in half.

● The unbreakable ribbon spun by the elves to hold Fenrir is made of a mountain's roots, a woman's beard, a cat's footsteps, a fish's voice, a bird's spittle, and a bear's sinews.

# Fafnir

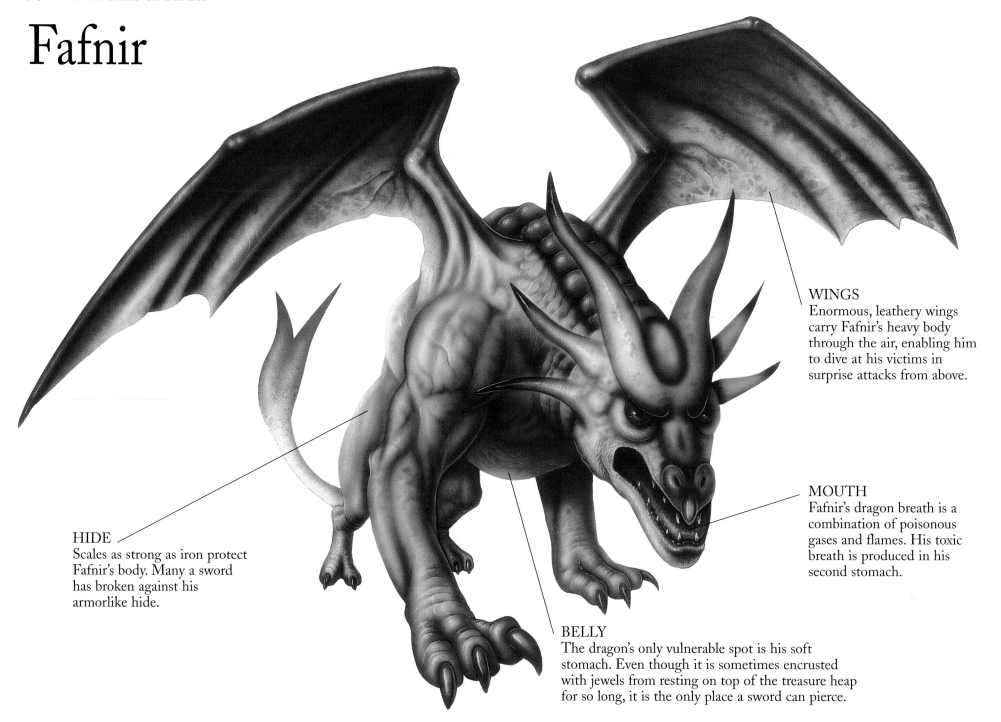

**WINGS**
Enormous, leathery wings carry Fafnir's heavy body through the air, enabling him to dive at his victims in surprise attacks from above.

**HIDE**
Scales as strong as iron protect Fafnir's body. Many a sword has broken against his armorlike hide.

**MOUTH**
Fafnir's dragon breath is a combination of poisonous gases and flames. His toxic breath is produced in his second stomach.

**BELLY**
The dragon's only vulnerable spot is his soft stomach. Even though it is sometimes encrusted with jewels from resting on top of the treasure heap for so long, it is the only place a sword can pierce.

Fafnir is a simple dwarf warped by greed. Fafnir and his brother Regin want a share of their father's treasure. Fafnir murders his father for the treasure and refuses to share with Regin. Years of gloating over his treasure transform Fafnir from a dwarf into a terrible dragon. Still hungry for a share of the treasure, Regin asks the hero Sigurd to slay Fafnir. The hero needs a reliable sword because the dragon's scales are impenetrable. Numerous swords have already shattered against them. Sigurd repairs his father's broken sword, making it unbreakable and sturdy enough to split an anvil.

SIZE

▶ SIGURD DIGS A TRENCH ACROSS THE PATH Fafnir follows for his daily drink at the river. Hidden in the trench, Sigurd thrusts his mighty sword into Fafnir's belly as he slithers overhead. At Regin's request, Sigurd cuts out Fafnir's heart and roasts it. Sigurd burns his fingers on the red-hot heart. When he sucks on his fingers to relieve the pain, the taste of Fafnir's blood gives Sigurd the power to understand the language of birds. The birds warn Sigurd that Regin plans to kill him, so Sigurd kills Regin and claims the treasure.

## Where in the world?

NORWAY ●

**According to Norse mythology, Fafnir crouches atop his heap of hoarded treasure in a cold, dark Norwegian cave.**

## Did you know?

● Until Sigurd came along, Fafnir was thought to be undefeatable. Numerous brave men went seeking the dragon's treasure but were burned alive and eaten.

● Fafnir's father was the king of Dwarf Folk. Several Norse gods gave Fafnir's father his treasure as payment for accidentally killing one of Fafnir's brothers.

● The sword that Sigurd has repaired in order to slay Fafnir was once his father's. It was broken when his father battled Odin, the chief god in Norse mythology. As his father lay dying, he predicted that his unborn son would one day forge a powerful weapon from the fragments of his broken sword.

# Sleipnir

**BACK**
Only Odin, the greatest of the Norse gods, can ride the swiftest of steeds. Any other rider on Sleipnir's back must have Odin's permission to be there.

**MOUTH**
Runes, which are ancient symbols with magical power, are carved on Sleipnir's teeth.

**BODY**
Lean, flat muscles in Sleipnir's shoulders and hindquarters propel his eight legs at high speeds.

**LEGS**
The swiftest of steeds has eight legs, one for each direction of the compass. His gallop cannot be slowed by water, air, or land.

Sleipnir is Odin's magical eight-legged steed. The greatest of all horses, and the swiftest on Earth, Sleipnir is the offspring of the shape-shifting god Loki and the horse of the giants. Odin, the chief god in Norse mythology, first sees Sleipnir as a colt being led by Loki with a rope. Odin admires the young horse, and Loki gives

SIZE

Sleipnir to him. He is the perfect mount for a god because no horse can keep up with him. Sleipnir can travel anywhere, galloping on top of ocean waves and over rainbows. He can also carry his rider into the land of the dead and back again safely.

► ODIN'S SON HERMOD RIDES SLEIPNIR FOR NINE DAYS and nights through a valley so deep and dark he could not see a thing. He rides into the realm of the dead to find his dead brother Balder. Sleipnir leaps over the vast iron gates into the land of the dead. The rotting dead all stare. Hermod strikes a deal with the ruler of the underworld for the return of his brother. If everything in all nine worlds, dead and alive, will weep for Balder, Hermod may take his brother home.

## Where in the world?

**In Norse mythology, Sleipnir may be found near Norway in the land of the gods, the realm of the dead, or anywhere in between.**

NORWAY

## Did you know?

● Hermod rides Sleipnir out of the land of the dead back to Asgard, the world of the gods. Hermod manages to convince every living and dead creature to weep for his brother Balder, with one exception. A single giantess refuses to cry, so Balder has to remain among the dead.

● Odin once rode Sleipnir to the land of the giants, where Odin bet his own head that Sleipnir could outrun any of their horses. Sleipnir easily beat even the fastest of the giants' horses.

● The bones of horses are often found in Viking burials. Horses were buried with their owners in the belief that they could carry their owner through the afterlife.

# Ziz Bird

**EYES**
The Ziz's eyes glow like
lanterns, making the bird look
as if he is lit from within.

**WINGS**
His wingspan is so great that it
slowly covers the Sun every
evening. The immense wings
enable him to flap quickly and
quietly across the world.

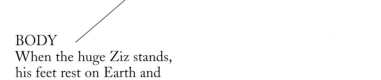

**BODY**
When the huge Ziz stands,
his feet rest on Earth and
his head touches the sky.

**CLAWS**
The Ziz can seize an ox in
his massive claws and carry
it great distances.

On the fifth day of creation, God makes the gigantic Ziz bird and orders him to use his tremendous wings to shade the earth and protect it from storms. The Ziz's enormous size is such a hazard that God instructs him to fly high above the earth. As king of the birds, he is responsible for protecting all flying, feathered creatures. A group of people spot the Ziz standing in water up to its

ankles with its head touching the sky. The people do not understand how large the Ziz is and assume it is safe to swim there. They are warned that the water the Ziz stands in is so deep that an ax dropped in it seven days ago still has not reached the bottom.

SIZE

▶ THE ZIZ SWOOPS DOWN ON A SHEPHERD'S LIVESTOCK ONE DAY and sinks his mighty claws into the back of an ox. As the Ziz lifts the ox off the ground, the shepherd grabs the ox's leg and is carried away. The Ziz transports the ox and the shepherd far away and drops them on top of a tower high above the sea. Later, when the Ziz returns to feast upon the ox, the shepherd cleverly ties ropes to the bird's legs so that he can hitch a ride with the Ziz away from the isolated tower.

## Did you know?

● The Ziz was fashioned out of marshy ground by God along with all the other birds of the earth.

● Once, a Ziz egg fell to the ground and broke. The fluid from the egg flooded several cities and crushed 300 cedar trees.

● The Ziz bird's presence reminds everyone to handle the forces of Earth with respect and care.

## Where in the world?

**Hebraic mythology of the Middle East states that the Ziz flies around the world to protect every bird in creation.**

● MIDDLE EAST

# Index